Dea

The   he St.
Ma   s calls
"th   nating
acc   ed the
national attention. St. Martin's is the publisher of Tina Dirmann's
VANISHED AT SEA, the story of a former child actor who posed as a
yacht buyer in order to lure an older couple out to sea, then robbed
them and threw them overboard to their deaths. John Glatt's rivet-
ting and horrifying SECRETS IN THE CELLAR shines a light on the
man who shocked the world when it was revealed that he had kept
his daughter locked in his hidden basement for 24 years. In the
Edgar-nominated WRITTEN IN BLOOD, Diane Fanning looks at Michael Petersen, a Marine-turned-novelist found guilty of beating
his wife to death and pushing her down the stairs of their home—
only to reveal another similar death from his past. In the book you
now hold, A DATE WITH DEATH, Michele McPhee examines a case
involving the Internet and murder which has made national headlines.

St. Martin's True Crime Library gives you the stories behind the
headlines. Our authors take you right to the scene of the crime and
into the minds of the most notorious murderers to show you what
really makes them tick. St. Martin's True Crime Library paperbacks are better than the most terrifying thriller, because it's all
true! The next time you want a crackling good read, make sure it's
got the St. Martin's True Crime Library logo on the spine—   u'll
be up all night!

Charles E. Spicer, Jr.
Executive Editor, St. Martin's True Crime Library

Titles by Michele R. McPhee

Heartless

A Date with Death

from the True Crime Library of St. Martin's Paperbacks

A DATE WITH DEATH

Michele R. McPhee

St. Martin's Paperbacks

A DATE WITH DEATH

Copyright © 2010 by Michele R. McPhee.

Cover photo of surveillance by *Boston Herald* / Polaris.
Cover photo of Philip Markoff by Mark Garfinkel / *Boston Herald* / Polaris.

All rights reserved.

For information address St. Martin's Press, 175 Fifth Avenue, New York, NY 10010.

EAN: 978-0-312-94506-0

Printed in the United States of America

St. Martin's Paperbacks edition / June 2010

St. Martin's Paperbacks are published by St. Martin's Press, 175 Fifth Avenue, New York, NY 10010.

10 9 8 7 6 5 4 3 2 1

For Riccardo

ACKNOWLEDGMENTS

I wish I could thank every law enforcement source and prison insider who helped me confirm facts about this case that have not been revealed publicly. Obviously, I cannot. Those sources know who they are, and I am in their debt.

I am grateful to my editor, Allison Caplin, for her resourcefulness—and unrelenting patience—under a very harrowing deadline. As always, I am honored to work with Charlie Spicer's stable of true crime writers. I must thank my agent Jane Dystel and my former editors at the *Boston Herald*, Joe Sciacca and Kevin Convey, for helping me nail down photographs. I tip my hat to my friend Norman Knight of the 100 Club of Massachusetts.

Most of all, *baci e abbracci* for *amore mio* Riccardo Passini, for his constant support and unmatched sustenance.

AUTHOR'S NOTE

I must point out that while Philip Markoff has been charged with Julissa Brisman's killing and other crimes, despite the evidence against him, he pled not guilty and, as of this writing, was awaiting trial. He had not, at press time, been convicted of any of the crimes discussed in this book.

1

Standing shirtless, Philip Markoff stared into the bathroom mirror of his comped hotel room in the Pequot Towers at Foxwoods Resort Casino in Connecticut and the words spilled out.

"I can't believe the bitch scratched me."

Markoff knew he shouldn't touch the sores, but his fingers involuntarily traced the angry red marks left on his chest by two acrylic fingernails, dug into his skin with unexpected strength and ferocity. *For a small girl, she did some damage*, Markoff thought to himself, staring at the wounds. At six-foot-three and 205 pounds, the twenty-three-year-old Markoff was solidly built but for the soft girth around the belly, extra weight he and many of his fellow Boston University medical students packed on as a result of a grueling schedule of study and hospital internships that left little time for the gym or healthy meals.

As he peered into the mirror, Philip noticed his blond hair was still tousled from the baseball hat he had been wearing earlier that night. The worn-out cap was his idea of a disguise. Not surprisingly, it would later prove to be not much of one.

With water from the tap, he smoothed down his hair, still worn in the same style he sported in high school, and then looked up again. His close-set blue eyes locked in on the scratches. Set against his pale-white skin, the red marks especially stood out, appearing deeper than they actually were. He used his meaty index finger to trace the wounds again and forced blood to the surface. As he absentmindedly smeared the blood together from the marks that criss-crossed his lower neck and upper chest, Philip Mark-off forced his mind to focus on what to do next.

Focus is what was desperately needed now if he wanted to avoid capture.

It wasn't supposed to have gone that way, not by a long shot. A woman who advertises herself through the Internet as a masseuse who specializes in "hand stress relief" was very low risk, no risk really, when it came to going to the cops if she got ripped off. When he had tried the same thing with another prostitute at another swank Boston hotel a few days earlier it had gone off without a hitch. Or so he thought.

But this time, things went off the rails. Completely. What caused this little girl to fight back? He had a gun for christsakes! *Why did that bitch scratch me*? It was not supposed to go this way.

After it was over and a young woman lay dead in a room on the twentieth floor of the Marriott Copley

Place hotel, Markoff left the hotel with his hat pulled as far down his face as his nose would allow. As he calmly walked through the lobby, he sent text messages to someone on his BlackBerry. Nonchalantly. As if the beaten, bloodied body upstairs did not matter at all. Then he scurried back to his apartment in the nearby suburb of Quincy.

He had no idea if anyone was following him or if anyone saw him arrive home shortly after midnight on April 15, 2009. But his first inclination was to get out of town. Panicked and bleeding from the scratches on his upper chest, Markoff pulled off his black zip-up jacket and hid the cell phone he had used to contact the masseuse. No one he wanted to hear from would be trying to contact him on it anyway. It was a throwaway, a prepaid disposable cell phone. He took off his loose black jeans and stuffed them in a laundry basket. The blue polo pullover he wore that night was never recovered. He then haphazardly stuffed some clean clothes into a duffle bag and headed south on Interstate 95.

He figured it was time to lay low for a while and he thought he had the perfect place—Foxwoods. It had certainly become a familiar place in recent months, his home away from home. He had visited nineteen times in the past three and a half months already this year.

Founded as a super bingo hall in 1986 and expanded under the Mashantucket Pequot Tribal Nation as a full-fledged casino six years later, the sprawling

4.7-million-square-foot resort in the woods of Ledyard, Connecticut, has grown into one of the largest casino resorts in the world. Millions of visitors flock to Foxwoods each year trying to capture "the wonder of it all," as their annoyingly catchy jingle used to intone, and beat the odds at one of its 380 gaming tables and 7,200 slot machines.

So at first blush, the perpetually crowded Foxwoods might seem a reasonable place to get lost in for a while.

But upon closer inspection, Markoff hardly could have chosen a worse place.

Instead of disappearing off the grid for a few days, Markoff, though not a suspect in the murder of the young woman found bloodied and beaten, half in an expensive room of a tony Boston hotel with her head in the hallway, was nevertheless under constant surveillance. The casino's sophisticated security systems recorded his every move, every dollar spent, every sip of soda. For a guy who wanted to vanish he could not have been more visible.

Markoff did not get the free room because he was a high roller. In fact, Markoff was strictly small-time, just another college frat boy who frequented the place from one of New England's colleges. He wore a weathered baseball cap, khaki pants and a button-down polo shirt, the uniform of all too many students who were living in Boston doing little other than pissing through their parents' money, their own trust funds or in some cases, their college loans.

No, the room was "comped" as part of a promotion. Markoff, a regular at Foxwoods, had applied for and received a Wampum Card and the free room came with it. The suite was nothing fancy; a standard room with scratchy comforters loudly emblazoned with multi-colored designs, a mini-bar, fridge and dresser, along with two queen beds and a flat-screen TV. In fact, he had stayed in similar rooms on his previous visits. He even applied for a line of credit . . . using his mother's address in upstate New York, of course. No need for that kind of paperwork following him to Massachusetts. Now it was April 15 and Philip Markoff was back at Foxwoods once more.

This visit, however, wasn't strictly to feed his gambling jones like the other times. On this trip, his freedom was at stake.

Markoff had the TV on in the background as he washed up in the bathroom. He was listening to the local news, wanting to know whether reporters had converged on the Marriott Copley hotel yet. A white woman shot dead in the ritzy hotel was a crime that was not going to stay quiet for long. It was going to be a big fuckin' deal for both the media and the Boston cops. He was certainly no criminal mastermind but he knew that much.

And once cops gathered all the facts, it was only a matter of time before the homicide was linked up to the carbon copy robbery of the hooker at the Westin Copley Place, another Boston hotel, two nights earlier.

Both women had checked into their rooms alone.

Both women came without any real luggage. And both women had advertised their availability for sex: one was a masseuse who specialized in "happy endings," or sexual release. The other was a hooker from Las Vegas with a long criminal history.

And once the cops connected the crimes, the next question would be could they tie Markoff to them. For all he knew, they already had. For all he knew they were taking the elevator up to his room right now.

Before he could make his next move, Markoff needed to know if the police had surveillance photos of the suspect who had shot the petite masseuse dead at point-blank range or if any incriminating evidence had been left behind. So he'd clicked on the television.

The newscasts that first night made no mention of surveillance pictures or evidence linking anyone to the murder. In fact, investigators did have surveillance photos, and they were pretty good ones at that. They had also quickly linked the murder to the robbery that had occurred on April 10. But the detectives were keeping that information to themselves for the time being. As far as Markoff knew, he was safe.

Markoff cleaned and covered his scratches. The injuries were only superficial but they nevertheless held the potential for ending his life as he knew it. The skin that was no longer on his chest and neck could very well be under the masseuse's fingernails just waiting for a medical examiner to remove them and make a DNA match. Markoff would have known all about DNA and autopsies through his studies. If they matched DNA from the crime scene to his, he was done.

Why did she fight back?

She was the one who put up a fight, the one who would eventually lead to his being arrested and humiliated. The one whose murder would uncover and make public in 36-point headlines a dark side he had managed to keep secret from his fiancée, Megan, from his family and friends and fellow students and even, in some ways, from himself.

Eventually, it would all come out; and it would all be used against him. The least of his worries should have been the skin under the woman's fingernails.

If the police could put it all together, Markoff could anticipate a rough time in the BPD interrogation room, not to mention an international media frenzy splashing his guilty secrets all over the world. His promising future as a doctor would certainly be smashed. His upcoming nuptials, which already gave him a sense of impending doom when he thought of the August 14 wedding day, would certainly never happen.

But as he checked in at Foxwoods, his secrets at least for now still his own, Markoff had a more immediate problem. How was he going to explain the marks on his skin to Megan, his fiancée?

At least for a day, he tried to put that question out of his mind. He took the elevator from his sixth-floor room to the casino level below, patting his pants pocket to make sure that the bills he had stolen from his victim the night before were still wrapped in a rubber band in his pocket. Comforted by the feeling of the cash, the bulge that assuaged his panic even if just for a minute, Markoff tried to bury the anxiety, the dread, and he went down to a blackjack table at the resort's latest addition to its sprawling compound—the MGM Grand. He slapped down $700 and traded the cash for seven black chips, each worth $100.

Then he sat down at a blackjack table, placed the pile of black chips on the felt. Less than two days removed from leaving a hotel where a 25-year-old woman was fatally shot, he started to gamble. Less than four days since a woman who could not only identify his face, but had given cops his fingerprints, had accused him of stealing $800. And at least for the time being, his luck did change. Over the next two days, Philip Markoff beat the house odds and parlayed his stolen loot into what to him was a small fortune, $5,300. At least for another day, he was living the Foxwoods dream.

"Take a chance, make it happen. Pop the cork, fingers snappin'. Spin the wheel, round and round we go. Life is good, life is sweet, grab yourself a front row seat and let's meet and have a ball. Yeah, let's live the wonder of it all . . . Meet me at Foxwoods."

2

In 2005, Boston's alternative weekly newspaper, *The Phoenix*, dubbed the Boston Police Department "The Worst Homicide Squad in the Country." It based that damning headline on the fact that the BPD homicide detectives were making arrests in only about a third of the city's recent murders, and of that, nearly 27 percent of the cases that went to trial ended in acquittal, compared to a national average of only 6 percent.

Based on those statistics, the odds may have seemed like they were tilted in favor of any wanted man, like Markoff, getting away with murder. But this wasn't your run-of-the-mill street killing and whether the BPD was in fact the "worst homicide squad in the country" or not—and most crime reporters in the city believed that the cops were not the problem that led to the negative story—the last bet Markoff wanted to make was that he could outsmart a veteran detective during what was sure to be a no-holds-barred interrogation.

The *Phoenix* was notoriously liberal and had a reputation in Boston for cop-bashing. In fact, many in the upper echelons of the Boston Police Department believed that the homicide unit was hampered by a glory-seeking district attorney named Dan Conley who heaped all the blame for a low clearance rate on the over-burdened detectives who were restricted by his policies when it came to issuing arrest warrants and prosecuting cases. Conley was the city's top prosecutor, thereby the top law enforcement official in Boston. Conley was a career elected official, one some lifelong Massachusetts residents might call a "hack." A hack in the Bay State was a lifelong politician who, once elected, had little worry about upcoming reelections because it was next to impossible to unseat an incumbent, especially a Democratic one. Consider that Edward "Ted" Kennedy was a United States senator for 47 years before he died in 2009. His colleague John Kerry has been a U.S. senator since 1985 and shows no sign of leaving. Congressman Barney Frank has also served Massachusetts for decades. Even the mayor of Boston, Thomas M. Menino, was elected to a historic fifth term in office in 2009. He had been running City Hall for fourteen years when he won again in a landslide victory, making him the longest-serving mayor in Boston's history. The incumbency stronghold was shaken on January 19, 2010, when Massachusetts voters sent the first Republican senator to Washington, D.C., since 1997. That man, Scott Brown, was a pro-law-enforcement candidate and many saw his election as a way to regain some control over the liberal ways in which criminals were coddled in the Bay State.

Conley, in fact, had his eye on Menino's seat and spent much of his career as the head of the Suffolk County District Attorney's Office raising money for his campaign coffers to mount that run.

As a result, Conley was despised by many Boston police officers and had garnered a reputation for bolstering his own statistics for "wins" by only prosecuting sure things and shelving cases that were not easily proven. The tension between the police and the prosecutor's office made it difficult to put bad guys away in Beantown. Another factor was the plethora of woefully inept judges, who, ironically, were appointed by the career politicians. The career politicians were known to use the campaign contributions made by attorneys to their reelection coffers as a gauge as to what kind of judge the contributor would make for the Massachusetts judiciary. Many of the judges were there because of politics, and not because of their qualifications. Most of the Massachusetts judiciary did not even bother to post resumes on the court's official website. No need. They were accountable to no one and they had some of the best pensions in the state. The only civil servants who earned a better pension than the judges were the politicians. Like Dan Conley.

All of it together created a belief for many in

Boston that one might be able to get away with murder, or at least have a better than 50-50 shot at it.

But the day after 25-year-old masseuse Julissa Brisman was murdered, Philip Markoff had an even more immediate concern than outsmarting the Boston Police Department and its much-criticized homicide squad.

He had to figure out how to justify the scratch marks that criss-crossed his chest to his fiancée, Megan McAllister.

The only way, of course, was to lie.

It would not be the first time he lied to his fiancée. Actually, he had become quite astute at making her believe pretty much anything he told her. It's not that Megan McAllister was stupid. In fact, she too planned on attending medical school. The key for Markoff was he had learned how to make Megan McAllister feel special. And he worked hard at it. He would bring her breakfast in bed. Nearly every Friday night, he'd buy fresh flowers. He helped her clean their apartment without being asked and caressed her head as they fell asleep. He was affectionate and attentive. A million little acts of kindness. What he got in return for all his effort was Megan McAllister's unwavering love, loyalty and trust. In fact, the depth of Megan's love for Philip would go on display for all the world to see less than a week later.

It was an exciting time for the young couple, what they both expected to look back on as their salad days: the lean, romantic time before the prosperous years that were sure to follow. They had it all. They were attractive. They had friends. Megan was svelte and could not wait to be married. Philip was handsome and would be serving his residency at one of the best hospitals in the world before long. They were the perfect couple. Each considered the other the perfect fiancé.

They joked about the low-rent building where the two aspiring doctors lived next door to the suburban riff-raff of one of Massachusetts most noticeably blue-collar towns—Quincy. Quincy calls itself "the City of Presidents," because John Adams and his son John Quincy Adams were both born there. But the last president to come out of the city just south of Boston finished his first and only term 180 years ago. Today, Quincy is solidly middle-class, decidedly blue-collar. But Megan McAllister's tastes and expectations ran much more blue-blood than blue-collar. She had no doubts that her exceptionally intelligent, if a bit geeky, fiancé would in due time get them out of Quincy and into one of the state's more elite zip codes like Wellesley or Weston or Newton, somewhere more fitting for a handsome young doctor and his striking wife. Maybe, they discussed, they could get a home in John Kerry's neighborhood of the Back Bay and Philip could walk to work at Massachusetts General Hospital. Kerry, after all, kept his neighborhood beautiful. So much so he had a fire hydrant removed from the front of his multi-million-dollar townhouse because it was "an eyesore" and his wife, ketchup heiress Teresa Heinz, had been tagged numerous times parking in front of it. Local newspaper photographers had also bagged pictures of her Jeep with the vanity plate Hnz57—as in Heinz 57—blocking firefighter access to the hydrant. The couple paid to have the fire hydrant moved around the corner.

Megan McAllister didn't mind that some people ridiculed the power couple for the move. Who didn't want neighbors who could throw their weight around like that? Philip assured her that it would only be a matter of time until they were out of low-rent Quincy and living large. But secretly he wondered whether he really belonged in the tony, sophisticated enclaves where Megan was already mentally constructing the McMansion of her dreams and laying out the blueprint for their future. The more time he spent with Megan McAllister and her expectations, the more he felt like an imposter in her world. Though they both grew up in small towns, simply put, they came from vastly different places.

Her family was a traditional, exceptionally close one: father, mother and three protective older brothers. She grew up in a borough of 6,100 called Little Silver, in Monmouth County, New Jersey, which, according to the borough's website, is "only a stone's throw to New Jersey's beaches." The McAllisters are like most people in Little Silver, which is overwhelmingly (97 percent) white and where the median household income is close to $100,000 a year.

Philip grew up in a small town masquerading as a "city" in the middle of New York State. The city of Sherill, all two square miles of it, is known for one thing: With 3,147 residents, it's the least populated city in New York State. Not much for the Sherill Chamber of Commerce to hang its hat on.

Like Little Silver, almost everyone in Sherill is white, more than 98 percent of them anyway. But the incomes of the people Philip grew up with were less than half, about $48,000 per household, than those of the people from Megan's town.

Philip also had a more fractured home life than his fiancée. Before college, Philip lived with his mom and stepfather while his big brother lived with their biological dad. There was love in the family but also tension and distance.

Whereas the holidays at Megan's house were festive and something to be looked forward to, the trips back to dreary Sherill to see his extended, semi-dysfunctional family always filled Philip with a sense of impending doom. For Markoff, family get-togethers were something to endure, not enjoy.

Ironically, Philip's mother worked as a cashier in a casino shop, though boyhood friends say that the young Philip never gambled in her casino. His father was a dentist with a practice in Syracuse. The couple divorced when he was still in elementary school.

By many accounts, Philip was one of those kids who grew up uncomfortable in his own skin, a mama's boy of sorts. Even if he didn't totally deserve that rap, his father didn't help him toughen up at all. His dad was a nice man, but a country bumpkin, one of those guys who let his neighbors get dental work on the cuff but was too insecure to ask them to pay up even when months had passed. What made it worse was that when his father got nervous, he began to rock back and forth completely unaware of his surroundings. It was embarrassing. Behind his back, Philip Markoff's classmates would joke that his father was "like Rain Man." But even if they had said it to Philip's face he probably would not have fought back. Markoff grew up with his mother, Susan, a robustly built woman who was shy and soft-spoken, and the stepfather-banker she married, Gary Carroll. They had a little girl together but their marriage would not last either. Still, in some ways Carroll was more of a father to Philip than his own father. His mother was nondescript, a woman who blended perfectly into the suburban sprawl of Walmart shoppers in upstate New York. A woman who wore cheap sneakers long after the scuff marks made them inappropriate for anything other than gardening. She preferred loose sweatshirts over black polyester pants. She did not have a shapely haircut and instead wore it short and unstyled. Megan McAllister's mother was stylish. The black pants she wore were tailored to her slender frame; her hair was coiffed at upscale salons on the New Jersey shore. The two women could not be more different. Megan's father cut an imposing figure, a man who commanded respect. He would eventually have to come to his daughter's defense and he did it with dignity. That's something that Philip's father just couldn't muster: a sense of self.

When he was small, Markoff lived in a colonial house on Thurston Terrace. Today, the backyard remains pristine and the paint job on the gray house is still impeccable. The Markoff clan that lived on Thurston Terrace has long since scattered. His father moved to nearby Lafayette, New York, taking up residence in a rambling two-story home. His mother lives alone in an apartment building called the Oneida Community Mansion House, which is anything but a mansion. Oneida was another small town whose only claim to fame was that the famous Oneida silver was once manufactured there. His stepdad, who divorced his mother, lives in a house by himself in Sherill. For reasons known only to them, Markoff and his brother stopped talking. In fact, by the time Markoff entered medical school he had no idea where his brother and his brother's new wife were living.

The first time the siblings would see each other in several years would be in a Boston criminal courtroom.

That this small-town kid from a fractured family made it into medical school, let alone that he was an excellent student with a seemingly promising career in medicine, seemed to be a minor miracle in itself.

Markoff was fully aware it was either a staggering accomplishment or an amazing stroke of good luck that he was even accepted into the medical program at Boston University, a prestigious school in Massachusetts, arguably the state that is home to the nation's best hospitals. Philip Markoff was not one of those "legacy" students whose well-to-do parents put medical textbooks in his crib and lectured him over country club dinners about the importance of MCAT scores. He was what Malcolm Gladwell might have identified as an "outlier" in his bestselling book by the same title. Philip Markoff was someone who had achieved success outside the norm, despite obstacles put into his path, outside of statistical probability. Frankly, Megan should have been the Boston University medical student and her fiancé should have been the one taking care of their domestic needs.

The bookwormish Markoff was a big kid but far from a schoolyard bully. Bespectacled and pock-marked, Philip was large but not imposing. He walked with his back hunched forward slightly. It was as if the weight of his fractured-up family and the pressures of staying "the perfect kid" pulled him forward.

Being a kid was not easy for Philip Markoff, but it wouldn't last.

Markoff was one of those teenagers who came back to high school from the summer break between junior and senior year and looked like a grown man, a muscular six-foot-three-inch man at that. He wore his

wavy blond hair intentionally tousled as if he had
just spent the day riding a motorcycle or navigating
nonexistent waves surfing Rockaway Beach in Queens.
Coupled with his intense blue eyes and broad shoulders, Markoff was movie-star handsome, just in a
nerdy kind of way.

Despite possessing a physique that should have
made him a gridiron star, the only sports he listed in
his yearbook were golf and bowling. Bowling. It was
a sport that may not have been considered popular
since candlepins actually made it to television in the
1970s, but Markoff took it very seriously. He was a
member of the bowling club. And he was a brain.
He had made his way into the National Honor Society and was a member of the history club. By then
Markoff had become a reclusive type of teenager
who excelled in his studies and who hung around
with the computer nerds.

Markoff had a quick wit—even if some of his
friends found his humor offensive toward women
and people who came from ethnically diverse backgrounds. He was fond of saying that he may have
been screwed in the sperm lottery when it came to
his broken and broke family, but somehow he managed to wangle an appealing appearance out of his
lineage. The remark would give some pause, as they
tried to figure out if he was being conceited or self-
deprecating. He was someone who could confidently
push his hand through his wavy hair and with that
one move command the attention of women twice

his age. The mothers of many of his friends enjoyed a harmless flirtation with this man-boy.

Meanwhile his own mother worked as a clerk at the Turning Stone Resort & Casino in neighboring Verona in scenic Mohawk Valley. The casino now boasts 2,400 Instant Multi-Games, a type of slot machine, as well as all the traditional games of chance: poker, blackjack, craps, etc. Turning Stone is one of those casinos that looks good in its advertisements but offers keno, bingo and "wagers starting at just one penny!" In the casino world, it is strictly small potatoes. Nevertheless, for kids from small towns like Sherill and Vernona, it had to have been the most exciting thing around. Was it his mother's job at Turning Stone that started Markoff's fascination with gambling? Though Markoff and his high school friends played a lot of poker, they later told reporters Markoff never gambled at his mother's casino. However, it can't be disputed that a few short years after leaving tiny Sherill, Markoff's life revolved around three things: study, Megan and gambling. And not necessarily in that order.

After graduating from Vernon-Verona-Sherill High School with honors, Markoff attended SUNY Albany where he was praised for his brilliant mind. During his college years he indulged in poker nearly every weekend, often all night. He was a bitter loser and not one to walk readily away from a losing streak. James Kehoe, a friend from Albany, told reporters that in addition to poker, Markoff liked video games and golf. He was essentially a typical college student. On the other hand, Kehoe related, Markoff was an intense student who drove himself to match his father's success. He might not have been close to the dentist from Syracuse but he still wanted his father's respect.

Markoff kept his darker side and habits under control throughout his undergraduate years, excelling academically and devoting himself to respectable extracurricular pursuits. Another roommate, Ryan Meikl, described Markoff as high-strung and intense. Markoff would get into heated debates about his support of the war in Iraq and was a supporter of gun rights. College classmates in Albany remember him variously as reserved or arrogant, and absolutely uncomfortable with any women until he met Megan McAllister.

Megan was two years older than Philip. It was an unlikely pairing from the start. She grew up a wealthy liberal Democrat and Markoff was a staunch Republican and a member of the College Republicans club at SUNY Albany. Markoff's political affiliation wasn't an easy label to wear on a liberal college campus. Being a Republican in Massachusetts would be even tougher. Some people in the notoriously liberal Bay State would sooner accept a murderer than they would embrace a right-winger.

"Markoff was a traditionalist," his classmate and fellow College Republican club member Jonathan Zietler told the *New York Times*. "Especially as far as things like men's and women's roles in society. He was a throwback to a more conservative era."

Megan McAllister would fit that ideal perfectly. She belonged to the same fraternity, Phi Delta Epsilon, and also had dreams of becoming a doctor. They were both community-oriented, volunteering at a local hospital. Sure, it was not completely altruistic. They did get college credits. But it was a way in which they could share stories about the craziness of an emergency room as they fell into bed after a long day pushing stretchers carrying patients.

On the Markoff-McAllister wedding website, Megan later detailed the start and evolution of their relationship. She wrote, "How We Met: We met going to college at University at Albany together. . . . Our apartment buildings were right next door and we didn't know it until one day we met at the hospital. We both started volunteering at the hospital on September 19, 2005. We volunteered at the Emergency Room together and spent about 2 weeks pushing stretchers down hallways and bringing blood and urine samples to pathology together before our first date on November 11, 2005!!"

Back then, it was Megan who asked Philip out, not because he was reluctant to date her but because he was still awkward with himself and lacked the confidence to approach such a beautiful young woman. Sure, it smacked of hypocrisy given the roles that he attributed to women. But after all, he was still the nerdy guy from a broken family whose high school career revolved around the bowling club instead of a football team. Megan was sophisticated. And even though she asked him out, she was a traditionalist and came from the type of family that Philip himself always wished he had.

Three years later, having been accepted to medical school, Markoff was a different man. Dropping to a knee during a horse and buggy ride on a crisp spring night in New York City on May 17, 2008, he proposed. On that night, Megan McAllister's entire life shifted from pursuing a medical education on the Caribbean island of St. Kitts to becoming Mrs. Philip Haynes Markoff.

From the moment he popped the question, Megan loved the word *fiancé* even if Philip Markoff was uncomfortable using it. It was a word she used at restaurants and with strangers they ran into in the hallway of their apartment. "This is my fiancé, Philip," Megan would say, accentuating the word that told the world not only was she was getting married but she was going to be a doctor's wife.

In many ways it was easier to focus on the pending wedding than on her own stalled career goals. Even though she came from a much more affluent background than her fiancé, it was Philip who was accepted to Boston University Medical School while she was turned down. In fact, the overseas school was one of the only ones that accepted her. And there was no way she was going to go to the Caribbean while Philip stayed behind in Boston. If she still wanted to be a doctor she'd have to obtain her medical degree at an embarrassing offshore school.

For the time being Philip could focus on his studies, she figured, while she would take care of the minutia of their wedding. Soon the big day became her all-encompassing obsession. For instance, on her website she set up trivia quizzes so friends could prove how well they knew the soon-to-be-wed couple. Which was odd, because Philip's family and friends had either never met Megan or if they had, spent a scant amount of time getting to know her. The same was true about Philip and Megan's friends. Some of her bridesmaids had only seen pictures of Megan's fiancé and had heard stories about him. Sure, some thought it was odd that they had never met Philip Markoff. But that was the way it went sometimes when people went their separate ways in college. Carl Maddalena, who lives in Little Silver, told reporters that his daughter Sarah was supposed to be a bridesmaid in the Markoff-McAllister wedding. The dad even knew that Megan McAllister had just bought her wedding dress. His daughter had known Megan since the girls were four years old. "This is such a shock," Mr. Maddalena said. "My daughter is trying to be as supportive as she can be." But even he conceded that it was odd that none of the bridesmaids had met Markoff.

Eleven different quizzes with pedantic questions like who designed Megan's wedding dress, "Priscilla of Boston or Vera Wang," graced the wedding site.

There was another about the location where Philip proposed and how he did it. There were inane, self-centered questions like, Does Megan prefer a cosmo or a cherry limeade to drink? She even asked her wedding guests and the nineteen members of her wedding party to weigh in on where she and Philip should go on their all-inclusive honeymoon: "Murrells Inlet, South Carolina; Saratoga Springs, New York; Boothbay Harbor, Maine; or the Mohegan Sun hotel and casino in Connecticut?" Philip preferred the last choice, for reasons that would not immediately become clear to his fiancée.

From the minute her engagement ring—a platinum ring with a single stone—was slipped on her finger, Megan transformed herself into a bride-to-be rather than a premed student. And she wanted everyone to know she was just fine with that supplicated role in life.

Megan McAllister knew what kind of life she wanted and thought that Philip Markoff was just the kind of man to provide it for her. In a way, she was right. That is, if the pressure of being the Philip Markoff that Megan McAllister envisioned didn't lead him to snap first.

First and foremost the storybook life she dreamed of with Philip had to start with the perfect wedding day. To ensure that it indeed was perfect, she became a bridezilla. She went so far on her wedding website as to set up a clock that ticked down the months, days, minutes and seconds until their August 14, 2009, ceremony began. A site that ticked down the months, days, minutes and seconds that were left of Philip Markoff's bachelorhood.

The wedding registry Megan created soon became filled with items that for someone from Markoff's humble background would certainly seem foreign and excessive and maybe even offensive. At the very least, some of the items were simply obnoxious. Others showed how naïve Megan was; how easy it was for her to build a life that she probably imagined since she was a little girl playing with her Barbie Dream House. In her new life as a married woman, Megan McAllister even wanted a pink kitchen, with a pink blender.

For example, of course, they would need fine china. Philip was going to be a doctor after all. But that would only be for big occasions. So they also needed everyday china and for that Megan picked out the Kate Spade Harbor set.

The rule of thumb for her wedding gifts was only name brands, recognizable, expensive brands at that. Especially Vera Wang: Vera Wang champagne goblets, Vera Wang sterling silver frames, Vera Wang serving utensils, Vera Wang silverware.

Plates and bowls and serving platters were also on the list, as if the soon-to-be Markoffs would be entertaining heads of state, or at the very least the heads of hospitals who could help her husband's advancement. The couple registered for expensive suitcases for all the world traveling sure to come. It was the wedding registry of a woman who envisioned herself entertaining the country club set, not the registry of a young and indebted couple, which they were. At the time, she wasn't working and Philip had already accrued $130,000 in school loans. The registry lacked the practical items that would be used by two people in their twenties starting a life together. Instead it was items that Megan McAllister very likely grew up with in her home on the New Jersey shore. Sure there was a blender (pink) and a Jack LaLanne juicer. Even a Krups coffeemaker. But those items appeared to be added as afterthoughts, located on the bottom of the list as if Megan realized that her other selections might strike some of her wedding guests as ostentatious, if not downright unaffordable. Even though the registry requests were made at Macy's and not Bloomingdales, they had an air of sophistication that was certainly not out of the ordinary for the McAllisters. But some of the items, like the $135 platinum creamer, might have struck the Markoff clan from tiny Sherill, New York, as more than a bit pretentious.

The Markoff-McAllister website told its wedding guests "We look forward to spending our special day with you" and included a picture of the couple that, in time, would be splashed on the front pages of newspapers across the country. But when it first went up on the website, no one looking at the happy couple, their faces tanned and smiling, could have guessed that anything but special days were in store for Philip and Megan. In it, Megan is leaning back into her strong, handsome fiancé's body, her head is cocked slightly to her right and her long, blonde hair cascades down over her shoulders. She is smiling comfortably and appears relaxed, despite the obvious posing involved in taking a picture. Philip is behind and to Megan's right a bit, his right hand resting tentatively on her right hip. His hair is cut short and neat. His smile, however, seems almost overly eager and gives him a much stiffer appearance than his beautiful, relaxed-looking fiancée.

Still, it's pretty typical fare when it comes to wedding-related photographs. The bride-to-be looks beautiful as "her day" approaches while her groom seems more nervous, just wanting the big day to be over with. In any event, there is no hint of the sociopath that prosecutors would come to accuse Markoff of being: the sexual deviant, the man who was capable of murder for money. If one were to read into it with the benefit of hindsight, the way Philip holds Megan, keeping her slightly away from his body even as it appears she is trying to fall into him, hints at perhaps a distance he is trying to keep between them. Or maybe not.

As Philip carefully cleaned and bandaged his wounds in his comped Foxwoods hotel room on April 15, Megan and her mother were in Little Silver working out the details of the sunset wedding ceremony that would take place on a beach in the nearby town of Long Branch four months hence.

Along with placing the china and other items on the registry, Megan was making arrangements with a Bruce Springsteen tribute band called BStreetBand to provide music. As anyone who has planned a wedding knows, there's a million things to be done and just when you think you've finished them all, up pops number 1,000,001.

Philip could not care less about china patterns and tea sets. When he saw that a creamer that they had registered for was made out of platinum and cost $135, he couldn't help but think of the old jam jars his mother used for juice glasses. One Kate Spade coffee mug went for $15. Of course they needed eight, according to the registry. A Vera Wang goblet was $35 each, and of course they registered for a dozen of them. Silver frames by the same designer were a hundred bucks. It was an opulent list, even if every purchase was offset by a small donation to the March of Dimes. But if Markoff thought his bride-to-be was going overboard, he kept it to himself. Like most grooms, he conceded that the wedding was to be Megan's day, not really his. Let her do what she wants.

He had other things on his mind.

3

Trisha Leffler was a prostitute and the johns she dealt with came in all shapes and sizes and dispositions. But they were never as young, good-looking or polite as the college student who came to her room at the Westin Copley Place hotel in the early a.m. hours of April 10, 2009.

She had flown in from Las Vegas early on Thursday and settled into a room on the thirteenth floor in the upscale hotel. Many hotels superstitiously skip from the twelfth floor to fourteenth, omitting designation of a thirteenth floor because some guest may associate the number with bad luck. Being on the thirteenth floor didn't both Leffler. She wasn't superstitious. Maybe she should have been. Or, considering that she left the room alive, maybe thirteen was her lucky number.

The john she was meeting that night found her through a posting she had on the website Craigslist.

In early 1995, Craig Newmark, an IT professional,

started what came to be known as Craigslist.org as an email list to friends and coworkers about upcoming events in San Francisco. According to the website, "What started as a fun side project in Craig's living room has since grown into one of the busiest sites on the internet, helping people with basic day-to-day needs such as finding a job, an apartment and a date, all within a culture of trust."

The site burgeoned from Craig Newmark's hobby into a site that receives 20 billion page views worldwide a month, 50 million of which are from U.S. residents. It has become a virtual location to find everything and anything, including whatever sexual acts you could imagine.

Under the headline "Personals," ads get placed on Craigslist for relationships such as: "strictly platonic," "women seeking women," "women seeking men," "men seeking men," "men seeking women," "misc. romance," "casual encounters," "missed connections," "rants and raves," and on and on. Criagslist has also become the perfect vehicle to peddle prostitution.

Leffler's ad, which offered that she was in Boston and asked "would you like to spend some time with a sweet blonde, give me a call," was located under the "casual encounters" category and included a cell phone number. She was careful not to include prices because that could draw attention from the law. Ordinarily time with "the sweet blonde" ran from $100 for a half-hour to $200 for two hours. Granted, "sweet blonde" may have been a bit of a stretch. Her time walking the streets of Las Vegas noticeably aged the once shapely Leffler beyond her twenty-nine years. She was five-foot-two and weighed about 135 pounds. Her hair was bleached blonde and the overprocessing had done some damage to her shoulder-length locks. She carried a little extra weight around the waist, which she blamed on her travels which came with a poor diet and an undesirable sleep pattern. The younger, prettier competition in Las Vegas had forced her to take her services on the road where she hopped from one hotel to the next in cities and towns all across the country meeting strangers seeking to spend time with a beautiful blonde. Of course, she was quick to tell police all she was doing was offering up "company" to lonely men. There was nothing sexual about it. But a cursory look at her arrest record in Nevada told a different story.

Leffler was quick-witted and had a way of making strangers feel at ease. She was aware that her job was unorthodox and people would judge her, but Trisha Leffler also knew she was good at it. And the bottom line was it paid the bills.

Her cell phone rang just after midnight on Friday morning, April 10. The caller sounded young. He said he was a college student. There was no talk of sex, Leffler would later tell police officers. But she did let him know what spending time with her would cost. He asked her, "What floor are you on?" When she told him, the caller joked, "My favorite number, thirteen."

Not long after the call, Trisha Leffler walked into the thirteenth floor hallway and met her "client" at the elevator banks. That was Leffler's idea of security precautions. If she didn't like the way the john looked, she told *48 Hours*, "I just tell him, 'no, thanks'" and then she'd walk away. She had certainly done it in the past. In her line of work you needed some street savvy, common sense and an ability to read people. She had acquired all of that, she would brag to police.

That night, the john waiting by the elevators gave no reason for such a reaction.

He was a tall blond man dressed in a black leather coat with an off-white shirt and a pair of expensive denim jeans. He did not meet her stare, and seemed aloof, but he was probably just nervous. College students looking for a quick hookup usually were. One thing was for sure, Leffler would tell investigators, there was nothing alarming about the way the tall blond guy looked in the hallway of the thirteenth floor of the fancy hotel room in Boston on that spring night.

"He was just a good-looking guy," she told the television show. "I mean, when I first laid eyes on him, I felt comfortable."

He followed her into her room. She slid the dead-bolt across the door and spun around to find herself staring down the barrel of a large black pistol. She had seen guns before but never one so close. From her point of view, it appeared to be humungous.

"Lie on the floor," the blond man said.

The sight of the gun set Leffler's heart pounding and she was so afraid she started to shake. She slowly made her way to the floor, unsure what the man, whom she had obviously misjudged, intended to do. Maybe this was part of a sex game, she told herself. Maybe the gun was a toy. Maybe he just enjoyed the look of fear in a woman's eyes. Her only option—no matter what this guy's story—was to go along with it. Whatever *it* was.

"I'm not going to hurt you. Stay still. Don't say a word."

As she lay on her stomach, the john stuck the gun in his pocket and gently pulled her hands, one at a time, behind her back. She felt his hands, they were soft, definitely not the hands of a working man. They were big but not at all calloused.

The man bound her hands with plastic "zip-tie" handcuffs, the type police use when they are making mass arrests.

Leffler tried to convince him tying her up was unnecessary. "You don't have to do all this. . . . You don't have to tie me up. You know, I'll give you whatever you want."

"Just be quiet," he told her politely, but sternly. He never raised his voice. He never engaged in expletive-laced tirades. To Leffler, it seemed that whatever he was into he had done it before. "No harm is going to come to you."

In an attempt to get him out of there as fast as possible, she told him that her pocketbook was in a drawer in the middle of the room's entertainment center. He found her purse and rifled through it, removing $800 and her credit cards. He asked her if she had any credit lines on the cards and she told him that they were all prepaid and there was no money left on them. Then he took out her bank card and asked her for the Personal Identification Number. When she blurted out a number, the man threatened that it had better be the right PIN or else "there'd be problems later."

When he shoved her purse into his pocket she asked if he could please give her her driver's license back and begged him to leave her at least one credit card so she could get home. The man quickly responded, "I thought you said they were all prepaid and there wasn't any money on them."

She stammered out an explanation that there was no money left on the cards but she could have people put more money onto one of them if need be.

Surprisingly he threw a card onto the floor next to her. A robber with a heart. He was going to take every dime she had, but leave her feeling all warm and fuzzy about him. Then he took her ID card, studied it as if, she thought, he were memorizing her home address, then also tossed it to the ground.

Next the handsome man asked for her phone. He started scrolling through her numbers and erased his number from the incoming calls log. Leffler wondered what the hell he was doing. He could erase the number from her phone, a BlackBerry Storm, but the phone company obviously could still trace the call. In fact, she could probably look up the number he used to call her online herself by checking the incoming calls on her phone bill. Then he turned the phone over and removed and pocketed the battery before tossing the phone to the ground.

Then the man walked over to her suitcase and started going through it. By now, Leffler was sitting up with her hands, obviously, still behind her back. He spotted a pair of her cream-colored thong panties on the ground and quickly picked them up and stuffed them in his pocket. He pulled out a knife and cut the room's phone wires. Then he started moving pieces of furniture around.

Leffler had no idea what this guy was up to. She thought it was weird but dared not say anything at first. Finally, she couldn't take it anymore. "What are you doing?" she asked.

"I'm trying to find something to tie you to," he responded. He said he needed to buy himself some time to get away.

She told him it was unnecessary. She wasn't going to call the police.

"I don't believe you," he said.

Finally, the man tied her to the bathroom door using the plastic ties. She heard him rummaging through her suitcase again (later it was determined he took more of her underwear) and then he ripped off three strips of duct tape and pressed them to her mouth. The introduction of the duct tape caused nightmare scenarios of S & M rape to run through Leffler's head and she started to panic again. But nothing happened. The handsome man told her that he'd call security in fifteen minutes and have them free her. Then she heard the door slam shut and he was gone.

Leffler was struck by how cool and calm the man was. "I mean, I'm not making presumptions but he was actually very calm. He basically knew what to look for, that kind of stuff," she told *48 Hours*.

But the robbery wasn't mistake-free.

At the beginning of the robbery, the man put on black gloves. But in order to secure Leffler's hands in the plastic zip cords and rip the duct tape, he needed to take the gloves off. Detectives later were able to take fingerprints off of several of the items used during the robbery as well as recover several pieces of Leffler's clothing which the man took as apparent mementos.

Leffler waited until there was absolutely no sound coming from outside the bathroom. Then she painfully squeezed her hands out of the zip-ties and ripped the duct tape off her mouth and threw the crumpled tape on the bed. She stood by her front door for maybe a minute, listening. Then she opened the door and quickly scanned the hallway, left, right, left. No handsome man.

She ran to the room next door and banged on the door. A doctor named James Earl Crowe, visiting from Tennessee for a medical conference, had been sound asleep when the pounding started. He was met by a disheveled blonde asking to use his phone saying she'd just been robbed. She wasn't crying but clearly shaken. She said, almost to herself, that maybe it wasn't the best thing to get the police involved. She went back and forth in her mind whether or not she should tell this stranger the truth about what happened. In the end, Leffler decided she was not going to let some college punk get the best of her. He took two days' pay right out of her pocket.

"I've just been robbed. I don't know what to do," Leffler told him. "I don't know if I want to call the police. I think he's gone."

The doctor was accustomed to reassuring nervous people and told her the best way to handle it was to call hotel security.

Within minutes security was at her door followed by two uniformed Boston police officers assigned to District Four.

"He was a tall blond guy and he pulled a gun on me," Leffler told the first two officers on the scene, Tim Lenane and Chris Holt. The officers exchanged glances.

Tall blond guy?

It was clear that the woman, "the vic," in this case had once been very attractive but that the streets had been hard on her. In good light, she looked closer to forty-nine than twenty-nine. She had gotten a little paunchy from a lifestyle spent on airplanes and eating room service in her hotel room. Her hair had been dyed so often it had become coarse. To the cops she looked like what she was, a prostitute, so they couldn't help initially being a bit skeptical of her story. They had heard it before in hotel rooms just like this one. A john refuses to pay. A "pros" or prostitute becomes a "vic."

Sure, she still looked cute in the short black dress, which some officers would later note was short enough to reveal that she had not bothered to replace the panties that her assailant had stolen. This inevitably lead to some joking back at the stationhouse comparing Trisha Leffler to the Sharon Stone character in *Basic Instinct*. It was a detail that was hard not to notice, especially for someone trained not to miss anything in a witness description. The lack of underwear led the officers to once again consider whether they were responding to something they had seen all too many times before: a prostitute who was stiffed on her fee, not actually robbed, who then turned around and cried robbery to get even with the john.

But then the victim showed them where the zip-tie still dangled from the bathroom door. She had wriggled free by forcing her small fingers into a tiny fist. Her wrists were still raised red from the indentations of the plastic restraints. Her right wrist had begun to bruise. Then they spotted the crumpled tape on her bed. The cops had to concede that it looked pretty legit, even if the description of the perpetrator didn't sound like the usual suspect. Instead the robber she described sounded like one of the thousands of college students who flooded into Boston each September with their trust funds and preppy clothes.

Lenane and Holt cleared the area to preserve the crime scene. They acted so deftly—securing evidence that would become particularly important days later—that their sergeant would later write them up for a commendation. It would have been easy to completely contaminate the crime scene. The vic could have had second thoughts and fled. Hotel security could have tossed the crumpled tape or tampered with the zip tie on the door. Because of the young patrol cops, there was a fingerprint lifted off one strip of the duct tape; a perfect latent print that would be a match if they could track down the assailant. The cops called for backup and went to the hotel security office to review videotape of the guests coming in and out through a revolving door on Huntington Avenue.

There he is, Lenane said, pointing to a computer screen with a scratchy digital image that showed a roughly six-foot-three-inch blond man with a baseball hat pulled tight around his forehead, just like Leffler had described. They were surprised at how accurate her description was of the perp, or perpetrator. He wore denim jeans and a black zipped-up jacket, just like Leffler had described. His head was bowed low over his BlackBerry. A white T-shirt stuck out from beneath the jacket that Leffler told them about. The victim may have been a prostitute with a long string of arrests, but she was also telling the truth.

"Is that him?" Lenane asked the victim.

"Yup," she said. "That looks like him. He's tall, just like the guy. I didn't get a really good look at his face because he never took his hat off. But that's his build."

Then she added, just to ease the tension, "Not a bad-looking guy. Too bad he's a psycho."

Leffler had no way of knowing at that moment how true those words were.

Lenane and Holt worked alongside the Boston Police robbery unit. Reports needed to be written and evidence logged. Leffler's cell phone, the one that her attacker had left behind, would be seized and eventually marked: "Seized. Turned in as evidence."

The robbery and assault took place right after midnight. The assailant had a gun. It didn't matter what the victim was doing in the room. Everyone knew that the media would be following this. The report was written up within hours of the arrival time. Not a single delay. Even the weather, "clear-night," was noted. So was the lighting: "inside. Well lit." Trisha Leffler's home address in Las Vegas was noted. So was her contact number. The doctor's name and address in Nashville also made it onto the report with his age, forty-seven. The suspect's description was noted:

"Male; white, non-Hispanic. 6-04 with a medium build and blond hair. Wearing a black leather jacket, tan zip-up sweater, jeans, brown dress shoes." Sometimes a witness will misremember clothing. Her description was close.

Leffler was lucky in more than one respect. Not only had she acquired a knack for remembering details (she had been through the robbed-by-a-customer routine in the past), but the detectives who responded to the scene were among Boston's best. One of them was Boston Police Sergeant Detective Danny Keeler, tall and impeccably groomed. Keeler was a man who was known throughout the city for his clearance rate—or how many bad guys he locked up in connection with crimes—and for his soft touch with victims. A longtime homicide investigator, he had recently transferred to the robbery division of District D-Four, a ramshackle police station in Boston's South End. Keeler would take charge of the secondary report that would be written about the case, one that would prove critical. The report noted two uniform cops who would come to be recognized for their astute handling of the case.

"Robbery, firearm; 10 Huntington Avenue; Room 1307.

"Dispatch time: 12:46

"About 00:46 on 4/10/09 Officer Michael Pankievich along with several other D-4 units responded to R/C for a robbery in progress at the Westin Hotel, 10 Huntington Ave. On arrival, the D904, Sgt. Doris took command of the scene. Crime Scene Unit notified and responded and processed the scene under the direction of D-4 detectives. Victim declined medical attention at the scene. To be further investigated."

The suspect was described as a white male roughly six feet tall, blond hair, black jacket, blue jeans. He did not appear rattled as he walked out of the hotel text-messaging on his BlackBerry.

Leffler would later say that as the robbery progressed she became less and less worried that the handsome man would hurt her. It was just a gut feeling. "I had a feeling he was just there for the money, he just wanted the money and to get out." She figured if he was going to rape her or torture her or kill her he would have done it right away. Not taken his own sweet time, as he did. And he wouldn't have been so quick to put the gun away. Leffler also suspected that he didn't think she would call the cops, given her chosen field. He gave her a credit card, let her keep her ID. He wasn't careful about making sure his fingerprints were not on the duct tape. He didn't even pull the gloves on until they were well into the attack. It seemed strange, but in a weird way Trisha Leffler had a begrudging liking for her assailant. She felt lucky he was so nice to her.

In a matter of days she would realize that she had escaped a bullet with the handsome college boy who showed up on the thirteenth floor that night. Literally.

Four days after she was robbed, Boston police detectives asked Leffler to look at another set of photos taken off security videotape. They were much clearer than the ones she had viewed from the Westin Copley's security system and she identified the robber immediately. It was the handsome man. In fact, he was wearing almost the same exact clothes. So Leffler asked if the pictures were taken from the night she was robbed.

" 'No, that's actually from the Marriott,' " she recalled the detective telling her. " 'There was a girl murdered there last night and we think this is the same guy.' "

At that point, Leffler suddenly changed her mind about the handsome man who tied her up and politely robbed her. It was then that the idea of who had come into her room chilled her to her very core.

"It dawned on me," she told *48 Hours,* "that he could have very well killed me."

4

On April 14, 2007, two years to the day before she traveled to the Boston Marriott Copley Place hotel to meet a client named "Andy" who had contacted her via Craigslist, Julissa Brisman finally felt like she had "arrived."

"I woke up on April 14 and said no, I can't do this anymore," she wrote in her diary. "I'm turning 24 in two weeks and I need to change!"

In their book simply titled *Alcoholics Anonymous*, which is more readily known as "The Big Book" among recovering addicts and twelve-steppers, AA founders Dr. Bob Smith and Bill Wilson used the term "arrived" to describe the epiphany some alcoholics have that it's finally time to quit. It was also a description that Bill W. used to describe the feeling of euphoria that accompanied the sound of an ice cube against the glass, the amber pour of the first drink. The cacophony of sounds that greet someone as they walk into a busy bar.

Smith and Wilson met in Akron, Ohio, after drunken benders in 1929 and eventually created Alcoholics Anonymous, which the Dalai Lama has since called the largest spiritual movement of the twentieth century.

Almost eighty years after AA was founded, Brisman was glad to be a part of it. For the first time in her life, Brisman was being introduced to a higher power, a God that she felt she could understand. And for the first time in a long time, she started experiencing what had become a foreign feeling—happiness.

Up until then, Brisman had always been able to get by in life on her looks. She was leggy and raven-haired, with a perfect pout. Her friends said she'd asked a Manhattan dermatologist for lips "like Angelina Jolie" and he gave them to her. Her physique was perfectly toned and she had a way of disarming people with a direct stare. Julissa's looks would attract men but something else moved them. Beneath the tough-girl exterior, she exuded vulnerability. A lot of men she met instantly felt a desire to take care of her—be her knight in shining armor.

Julissa Brisman was a woman who could certainly handle herself in a tough situation but in some ways also seemed defenseless. Because of that men felt the desire to protect her from the world and sometimes from herself. For years Julissa struggled with drugs and alcohol. The addiction did not grip her every day, but when she put booze or a drug into her system it was as if a devil had been unleashed.

That's when she couldn't stop. The compulsion had been set off and that's when Julissa would find herself in a danger zone. Binging, blacking out, losing expensive shoes, waking up naked in the beds of strangers. It was a nightmare life and one that she didn't want for another minute.

But her chaotic, reckless life came to an abrupt and unexpected end on April 14, 2007. That date would become so important to her, such a watershed moment in her life, she tattooed 4/14/07 on her ankle. On that day someone took her to an AA meeting and it changed what remained of her life. Julissa attended her first Alcoholics Anonymous meeting in the trendy Soho neighborhood of New York City in the not-so-trendy basement of the Church of St. Antony Padua. It was absolutely packed. Expensive motorcycles and luxury cars were parked all around the church. Clusters of very attractive people—some recognizable as movie stars and models—mingled outside, smoking cigarettes and trading war stories. Julissa did not know what to expect when she descended the stairs into the room that was used as a bingo hall at other times during the week. She was surprised to see so many familiar faces, people made not only famous from the big screen or magazine spreads but infamous from the reports of their drunken or drugged-out public antics. But substance abuse is the great equalizer. The bold-faced names who attended that AA meeting might be considered "stars" to the outside world, but once they sat down on those uncomfortable metal folding chairs in the basement of St. Anthony Padua's they were just another drunk or druggie. No better or worse than anyone else in the room. No different, in fact, than Julissa herself.

In any event, Julissa had the looks and style to keep pace with any of the so-called beautiful people in the room that Friday night. She was wearing an ensemble she had picked up at Prada earlier that week. Despite her anxiety, her hair was still shiny and styled and her makeup was perfectly applied. She looked fantastic.

Out of all the AA meetings Julissa could have attended as she took her first steps toward sobriety, the Friday night Soho meeting was perfect for her. As stunning as she was, at St. Anthony Padua's she could attend the meeting without standing out too much. The other people were equally attractive and also well-dressed. Somehow that made her feel much better. It also made her more apt to listen as they took the podium at the front of the room and shared their "experience, strength and hope." The fear that her life would be over—boring, mundane, routine—if she got sober quickly evaporated. She liked coffee and people here sure drank a lot of it. She also liked attractive people. And she liked the idea that some addicts could replace booze and drugs with caffeine, sex and shopping.

There was something else that attracted Julissa Brisman to what was happening in that basement room that night. It seemed to her that most of the people in the room were happy. Something she had never been. They had a positive energy and seemed to genuinely like one another. More importantly, they liked themselves. For the first time in a long time, Julissa felt a sense of belonging. The panic that often plagued her without provocation and forced her to reach for a drink or snort a line of coke vanished as she sat there listening and watching. She took in a deep breath that night in a church basement bingo hall and knew innately that her life had just shifted. And it had. In AA parlance, Julissa Brisman had finally "arrived."

Like most addicts, Julissa did not get it right the first time. She had a couple of relapses but, according to her diary, hadn't had a touch of alcohol since September 19, 2008.

"I had a taste of the sober life, and I liked it," Julissa wrote in the last entry of her dairy, the cover of which was adorned with the prayer, "God, grant me the serenity to accept the things I cannot change; the courage to change the things I can; and the wisdom to know the difference."

The Manhattan neighborhood that Julissa grew up in was transitioning from what had been one of the toughest parts of New York City, the aptly named Hell's Kitchen, with a mishmash of Irish gangsters and new arrivals from all over, into what the real estate agents were cleverly soft-pedaling as Clinton Hill to the hordes of yuppies flocking to Manhattan in the 1980s. Hell's Kitchen was a real neighborhood. Tough but real. Clinton Hill was a realtor's illusion. But one that worked when it came to selling million-dollar condos.

Located on the West Side of Manhattan stretching from 34th Street up north to about the mid-50s, Hell's Kitchen was dotted with brownstones and high-rise tenement buildings. Famous and powerful gangsters like Bill Dwyer and Owney Madden, bootleggers during Prohibition, operated out of Hell's Kitchen. They were succeeded decades later by a decidedly less dapper crew of vicious drunken killers called the Westies. For the longest time, Hell's Kitchen was one of the real authentic New York City neighborhoods where people knew one another's names, old ladies hung off fire escapes and injected themselves into everyone's business and storekeepers pulled double duty by acting as neighborhood watchdogs. In those days a shopkeep wouldn't call the cops if he caught a kid stealing something from his shop, he whacked them with an open hand upside the head and barred them from his store for thirty days. Then he called their parents.

That era was quickly passing by the time Julissa was a coming of age in Hell's Kitchen. For better and worse, the yuppies had moved in by then and many of the old-timers were being priced out of their own neighborhood.

Author T.J. English explained what had happened to the old Hell's Kitchen in his book, *The Westies*.

"As a low income neighborhood in close proximity to the theater district and midtown Manhattan, Hell's Kitchen was ripe for development. In the late 1970s and early '80s, huge office towers servicing some of the most powerful law and advertising firms went up along 8th Avenue. Condominiums and co-op apartment buildings were being constructed to house the financial analysts, lawyers and investment bankers who now worked in the area. Inevitably, long-time residents were displaced."

While the gentrification ripped the heart and soul out of Hell's Kitchen, the criminal elements, like cockroaches, were harder to snuff out.

Throughout the 1980s and into the early 1990s, there was still a palpable toughness to Hell's Kitchen made famous in the Sean Penn movie *State of Grace*, about an undercover cop who was given the task of taking down a ruthless collection of Irish gangsters that he had grown up with. Much of the area when Julissa was growing up was still controlled by the Westies, an organized crime outfit of drug dealers and contract killers comprised of Irish tough guys who came under the tutelage of Mickey Featherstone and James Coonan. Julissa learned to watch her back. Make sure that a skinny, shaking junkie did not get too close to her. She walked briskly past alleyways just in case. She never went anywhere alone if she could help it.

Julissa Brisman was street-smart but she was also a follower of sorts. It wasn't long before her friends were drinking tall beers out of a paper bag on the corner. The booze would eventually spiral out of control and drugs like cocaine and Ecstasy would enter the party picture when Julissa was a teenager.

To pay for it, Julissa used her biggest asset: her looks. She never prostituted herself straight out. Instead, she would escort wealthy men to events. She would do stripteases and kiss other women at bachelor parties. Eventually, she moved into massages, sensual messages with "release," as they say in the business, a code for the sex act commonly referred to as "the happy ending," a hand job. Scantily clad in panties that she would purchase during her high-end shopping sprees, Julissa set up a one-woman business that sometimes brought in $1,000 to $2,000 a day. It was more than enough money to outfit her in the Chanel and Gucci ensembles that she preferred now that she had reached her twenties. The wraparound sunglasses that were an essential part of her look cost anywhere from $400 to $600 a pair. The more expensive her clothes were, it seemed, the better she felt about herself.

When she got sober, Julissa knew she wanted a better life. She wanted to help other women, who like her, struggled with addiction and low self-esteem. She enrolled in City College of New York as an undergraduate and entered the substance abuse counseling program run by the renowned recovery expert Jack Bennett.

Friends say she was trying to transition out of her

life as a masseuse and into substance abuse counseling. But that wasn't going to happen overnight and she still loved to dress in the best clothes and shoes money could buy. There were also still bills to pay. So Julissa continued to pick up the easy money to be made working as a "massage therapist," the "happy endings" justifying the means. Using the Internet, she advertised and found a hungry audience especially among men claiming to be lonely traveling businessmen. She would agree to meet them in hotel rooms all over the East Coast. First, she'd rent the room in an upscale hotel and settle in for a few days. She'd service her clients, then come back the next day with a few grand in her pockets. At $200 an hour, she was able to maintain the lifestyle she had grown accustomed to, pay for her schooling and put some money away on the side. And her clients got to go home happy. So who was it harming?

In between masseuse gigs, Julissa worked at her best friend and former roommate's tanning salon and was trying her hand at acting and modeling. She was also a member of the animal rights group, PETA, and had a dog that she was devoted to named Coco Chanel. Of course.

She was not the high-priced escort living in a luxury apartment that some stories would make her out to be. She shared a one-bedroom apartment in a Brooklyn neighborhood. Her room was adorned with a large Marilyn Monroe poster and a Marilyn Monroe calendar.

Her roommate, Max Kuperman, later told the *Village Voice* that Julissa would leave town for days at a time when she went on her masseuse gigs.

"I warned her about all the guys," he told the *Voice*. "I warned her so many times that she should watch out for all these perverts out there. I wish I tried harder."

But part-time work in a tanning salon wasn't going to keep Julissa in Prada. She was not ashamed of her penchant for the finer things in life. In fact, she emulated the well-heeled writer Carrie Bradshaw on the hit HBO series *Sex and the City*. The wildly successful show often centered on its star, played by Sarah Jessica Parker, shopping for $1,000 pairs of shoes. On her MySpace page, Julissa said she lived by a quote from the show, written by the onetime columnist for the *New York Observer* Candace Bushnell: "The most exciting, challenging and significant relationship you can have is the one that you can have with yourself. And if you find someone to love the you YOU love, well then that's just Fabulous."

Within hours of her writing that on her MySpace page it would be noted how ironic it was. Julissa was finally in a space where she did love herself. She had been "rocketed into the Fourth Dimension," as her beloved Big Book called the state when sober life has a way of becoming enchanting. Her worst day sober, Julissa liked to say, was better than her best day drinking. She had been given a new lease on life. She was living in the "sunlight of the spirit," as the Big Book described a spiritual awakening. She certainly had needed one. Sure, she worked jobs other than as a sex worker. In fact, while she was a clerk at Macy's there was an incident where she was accused of grand larceny. She pleaded guilty but her mother would tell *Vanity Fair*, "A girl stole clothes from Macy's, told them that Julissa knew about it, and then she disappeared. Julissa said the girl was lying. Julissa paid it all back." That happened in 2003, long before her newfound lease on life. She really wanted to be an actress and bragged about it: "ACTING . . . I live it . . . I breathe it—it's my Passion!" She crowed about fashion shows and Broadway and smaller theatrical productions. "I love SeXy TimEz—Hanging out and spoiling my GorGeOuS dOG CoCO ChAnEl! He's the Man of my life!! Oh ya!!!"

On that same MySpace page Julissa confessed to a deep-rooted attraction to "Ivy Leaguers," writing: "JuLissa thinks Ivy Leaguers are Adorabul-icious!!"

It would be her last entry on the social networking site. When she typed it she had no way of knowing it would be a preppy, Ivy League type who would be accused of ending her life on the very day of her last login: 4/14/09.

Yes, two years to the day after Julissa Brisman "arrived," having walked into the meeting she credited with saving her life, she was dead. And it was a man she probably would have described as "Adorabulicious" who would be accused of murdering her.

5

Joe C. was holding court at the Kowloon restaurant on Route One in Saugus, Massachusetts, with a group of other guys, guys like him who enjoyed the luxury of long leisurely lunches because their "jobs" were not demanding at the moment. Or pretty much ever, for that matter.

The men wore sweatsuits because the Kowloon was that kind of laid-back eatery. Still, the sprawling Chinese restaurant was so famous throughout New England that a wall inside the joint was covered from floor to ceiling with pictures of famous sports stars and actors and big-shot comedians, arms slung around the shoulders of the owners and staff.

Joe's BlackBerry vibrated in his pocket and chirped with the signal that he had a new email. He looked down at the sender and smiled. Joe did not consider himself a guy who frequented prostitutes or high-priced escorts. Not a whoremonger by any stretch of his imagination. He was just a man who liked the company of interesting women and if it came with a massage and a "happy ending," well, all the better. It was harmless enough. The hot brunette he knew as Morgan, the leggy, young thing who looked fantastic in a Cosabella bra and matching panties, was certainly what Joe C. considered an interesting woman. Morgan's "handler" had sent him an email. He was familiar with the "handler" too. Her name was Mary Beth Simons. Well, that was the name she used for business. Her other name was Beth Salomonis. It would never become clear which name was her real one.

Joe was very popular with women who worked as "massage therapists." He was robustly built and had a plethora of unsavory friends around him. But he was also gentle and extremely generous. Because of that he was on Mary Beth's "regulars" emailing list, entitling him to his pick of the best-looking girls and most desirable times. He read the email and a smile spread across his beefy face. It was going to be a good week.

"Hi! My girlfriend Morgan, the massage therapist will be visiting Boston Monday 4/13 (available from 1pm until 11pm); Tues 4/14 from 7am-11pm; and Wed 4/15 from 7am-12noon checkout!) *She Visits only once every 1-2 months so don't miss her! Her pics are real, recent, and attached to this message. She is visiting just these couple of days and I highly recommend her!* If you would like to schedule, PLEASE E-MAIL back SEVERAL TIME PREFERENCES that work for you during Morgan's window of availability and I will do my best to accommodate you. Be sure to INCLUDE YOUR PHONE NUMBER; I do not give out a contact number until you have provided yours! Kisses XOXO Morgan & Mary.

"PS- The rate is $200/hr for sensual massage inclusive of hand stress relief. Other sensual extras available and discussed in person at the time of the massage (for reasons of discretion). In call only, not full service. PPS- we are not currently advertising or accepting new clients . . . so please email and notify me personally before reffering [*sic*] a friend to email!"

Joe noted the misspellings in the message he repeated verbatim.

The pictures attached to the email took Joe's breath away. There was one with "Morgan" leaning over just enough to have her ample bosom spill out of her lacy black lingerie. Her pink thong was a startling contrast against her tanned skin. Her makeup minimal. "Morgan" had luxurious, long, full brown hair highlighted with just enough blonde to accentuate her olive tone. And that mouth, those full, Angelina Jolie lips. In another photo she was lying back on a bed in a hot pink bikini, her hips raised ever-so slightly, her hair draped seductively over one eye.

Joe planned to visit Morgan. Not because he wanted to unload two hundred for sensual relief, or so he says. He wanted to meet with Morgan because, he says, he found her funny and sweet. He liked hearing about her plans to become a drug and alcohol counselor and asked her about her college classes. He had known Mary Beth Simons for years and respected the fact that she was a businesswoman in New York who owned a tanning salon—the tanning salon where Julissa worked. Not because she needed the money, or frankly because Mary Beth needed the help. Julissa, like most of the tanning salon employees, was eye candy, enticement for the men who liked to get in a little electric beach time and ogle some gorgeous women in one brief salon visit. Mary Beth and Julissa were onetime roommates and had been close friends for years. Mary Beth was gorgeous, like Julissa, but she was smarter with money. Instead of buying expensive clothes, she invested in real estate and business ventures. The two made a good team. Where Mary Beth was serious, Julissa was adventurous. Where Julissa was irresponsible with her earnings, Mary Beth would make sure she squirreled enough of her money away to pay for her college courses.

On the morning of April 13, 2009, Julissa Brisman woke up in her room on the twentieth floor of the Marriott Copley. She later went to an afternoon meeting of Alcoholics Anonymous. Even when she traveled she kept her program first. It was also a good way to keep things going forward, make sure she didn't slip up and start drinking or drugging again. Besides, she liked the meetings. She felt connected to the people attending them. It made her feel good about herself, resolute about her life before she had to deal with her clients, guys who were sometimes creepy and always strangers. Men whom she'd soon be massaging then masturbating while dressed only in her lingerie.

At 5 p.m. Julissa logged onto her Facebook page. She chatted with friends and waited until it was time to start meeting with other clients. Back in New York, Mary Beth Simons received a text message from Julissa saying she had a client in Boston who told her his name was Andy. Julissa had never dealt with "Andy" before. He found her, "Morgan" that is, via her ad under "massage" in the Erotic Services section on Craigslist. He wrote to her from the email address AMDPM@Live.com. He said he was an out-of-towner. "I myself am visiting Boston and was looking for a 10 p.m. or later appointment tonight or tomorrow. Unfortunately I will not be free any earlier." Morgan emailed him back from massages bymorganboston@yahoo.com saying she was free that night.

"Andy" responded, "Morgan, I can still make it tonight but I am thinking tomorrow at ten would be better for me but otherwise I'll be there tonight as planned. Thanks, Andy."

Julissa wrote back that the appointment would work. "I could do it tomorrow night or we can do

10:30 or 11 tonight if you wanted to see me later tonight. Let me know what you prefer. Morgan."

He again wrote back. "Hey Morgan: 10 p.m. tomorrow is best for me. Thank you, Andy."

The next night, "Andy" dialed the number Julissa listed along with her Craigslist ad. Back in New York, Mary Beth Simons answered it. It was "Andy" and he was about twenty minutes early. Mary Beth told him to go to the room at 10 p.m. Then she sent Julissa a text and said her 10 p.m. had arrived and asked Julissa to text her when it was over. That was the system Julissa and Mary Beth set up. Call when it was over, that way Mary Beth would know Julissa was safe. It probably comforted Julissa knowing someone else knew where she was and ostensibly who she was with. But that was all the system was useful for. Mary Beth Simons was more than two hundred miles away in New York. There was no set time to push the panic button whereby if Mary Beth didn't hear from her friend she'd call the cops. For all intents and purposes, Julissa Brisman was on her own.

In addition to the fake name, Markoff had taken other steps to avoid detection. The medical student used a "throwaway" phone he bought for all his calls to "Morgan" and her handler. With regular cell phones, investigators can easily triangulate a suspect's location using the cell phone satellites and cell towers that connect the calls to hone in on the whereabouts of a specific cell phone user and the time that calls were made. This allows them to establish that suspects were close to the crime scene at or about the time the crime occurred.

But the phone "Andy" used, a disposable sold by TracFone, could not be easily traced because once the prepaid minutes were used up the client tossed it or recycled it. If the phone purchaser used cash to buy the phone then there was virtually no way of uncovering his identity. The phones are popular with drug dealers and gangsters and other people whose freedom depends upon the authorities not being able to monitor their comings and goings.

Markoff also used a phony name to set up the email account which "Andy" used to contact "Morgan." But unlike the throwaway phones, emails, even sent from phony accounts, leave trails that aren't so easily erased.

As 10 p.m. became 11, then midnight, then the a.m. hours started to tick by, the "job over" text message Julissa was supposed to send to Mary Beth Simons never came.

Joe C. never got a chance to chitchat with "Morgan." In fact, he never even knew her real name. The next time he would see a picture of the hot brunette who was studying to be an alcohol and drug counselor would be when he awoke to a front-page picture of her on the cover of his favorite newspaper, the *Boston Herald*. A pretty woman murdered in a fancy hotel room was front page news. Joe frantically dialed Mary Beth, but by then she was busy helping

Boston Police investigators track down "Andy," Julissa's last client. Her information would prove critical to detectives.

"Andy's" emails were like a bread crumb trail that would lead them to the Craigslist killer within a matter of days.

6

What should have been a day of celebration for Julissa Brisman was instead the day she was murdered.

The 911 call came at 10:11 p.m. on April 14, 2009. It had been two years, to the day and pretty close to the hour, since she walked into her first Alcoholics Anonymous meeting which eventually led to her sobriety.

Some in the sobriety circles marked the day with a cake—as if getting sober was a rebirth of sorts. In fact, some called it a birthday. Others an anniversary. But one thing almost always happened. The person marking the occasion that they had "arrived" chaired an AA meeting and collected a medallion at the end of the hour, a way to let newcomers know that it was possible to stay off drugs and alcohol "one day at a time," as they say. It was usually an emotional meeting, one that other alcoholics and drug addicts looked forward to. It was just so damn hopeful to think that people were able to stay sober first a minute at a time, then a day at a time, then a month at a time, until the years accrued. The days became months and the months became years and life just got that much better—sober.

On that day, Julissa did not want to miss an opportunity to make sure she raised her hand in a meeting and acknowledged her sobriety. Sure, she had had "a slip," the lingo used to describe a relapse, so technically it was no longer her anniversary or birthday. Still, it felt good. Every day without a drink felt good. She was on what many sober folks referred to as "the pink cloud." Life looked rosy without the filter of booze. It was cold, sure, but the chill felt good. Julissa walked to a noontime meeting not far from her hotel in Boston's glorious Trinity Church. The cold had invigorated her and the welcome she received from fellow alcoholics who were trying to stay sober one day at a time gave her spirit a rise. It was to be Julissa Brisman's last AA meeting. She had even called her mother after the meeting on the night she was killed. Just to hear her voice.

It was the last time Carmen Guzman would hear from her baby girl. That night Julissa told her about a man she met on the subway in Boston. A college student, she told her. Carmen Guzman had no idea, of course, what her daughter was really doing in Boston.

"Nine-one-one, this line is recorded," the operator said to the breathless security guard from the Marriot Copley hotel who called. "What is the location of your emergency?"

"One-ten Huntington Avenue," the security guard answered.

"One-ten Huntington Avenue?" the 911 dispatcher asked.

"Yes, the Marriot Copley hotel."

"Do you need fire, police or ambulance?"

"I just called for an ambulance but we are going to need BPD [Boston Police Department] here for a possible stabbing."

"This is in Boston, the Hotel Marriot, you said," the dispatcher asked.

"Yes."

"And your name sir."

"I'm in security," the man responded.

"And you said you already called this in?"

"Yes, we already called for an ambulance but we are going to need BPD here also."

"This is a possible stabbing, you said?"

"Yeah," the man responded. He then released an audible sigh.

"Stay on the line one second, okay, hon?"

"Yup."

"Do you see the person is stabbed, sir?" the dispatcher then asked.

"I actually have my supervisor up there right now. He actually said that she may have passed away. He's trying to evaluate what's going on up there," the security guard said.

"Okay, sir. She might have passed away, you said?"

"Yeah."

"And the female that EMS is already on their way for—you said it might be a stabbing?" the dispatcher asked again, trying to keep the caller on the line.

"A possible stabbing, yeah," he said. He then keyed up a portable radio. "Stand by. I'm on the phone with nine-one-one dispatch."

"Actually, if I'm not mistaken, units are already en route, hon," the dispatcher said in a thick Boston accent.

"Okay," the guard said. He was aware of the technique. Keep him on the line as long as possible in case he was somehow involved in what was sounding like a 911 call to report a homicide at an upscale hotel in Boston's toniest neighborhood, the Back Bay.

"I'm going to put this in and I'm going to also add that you said she's probably passed away, okay?" she said, stalling.

"Yes," the guard said. He stifled a sigh.

The first on the scene were firefighters from Engine 33. Their arrival time was 10:13 p.m. What they found was a woman wearing a bra and panties splayed out in the hallway—her brown hair matted. There was so much blood they guessed she had been stabbed repeatedly. Security had been summoned to the room by a Manhattan jewelry designer who was touring colleges with her teenage son when she heard what she later described to reporters as a childlike "shriek" coming from another room on the twentieth floor.

Within a minute, security found the body of Julissa Brisman. There was a zip-tie fastened to one of her wrists.

The security officer muttered under his breath, "Jesus Christ. Oh Jesus Christ." He fingered her small wrists, desperately searching for a pulse. He keyed his radio and called for another security guard to join him. There was a faint pulse.

Soon a Boston firefighter arrived and started CPR. EMTs then came racing down the hallway with a stretcher. Julissa was transported to Boston Medical Center.

In no time, the twentieth-floor hallway was swarming with Boston police officers from District D-Four and detectives from the elite homicide unit. Boston Police Sergeant Detective Danny Keeler immediately realized that this was similar to a more run-of-the-mill case he was investigating from a few nights earlier at the Westin down the street. The robbery of a prostitute named Trisha Leffler. Keeler was soon joined at the Marriott Copley by Lieutenant Detective Bobby Merner, a hard-charging investigator who was small and compact, built like a bullet. Merner was one of those cops whose name alone created a buzz among rookies and even some of the hardened rank-and-file. He was what they called "a squared-away cop." Sure, he was cantankerous, even downright nasty sometimes. But he was also respected because he would not stand down until the bad guy was caught. When he was in pursuit of a suspect, especially a murderer, Merner moved in as swiftly as a bullet and had the bracelets fastened before the target knew he had even been eyeballed. Merner and Keeler were not rivals but nor were they friends. Both men had come up in the ranks racking up arrests that solidified their reputations as dogged investigators but they also alienated some of the officers who resented the way they worked. Keeler and Merner were the types of cops that were either loved or loathed depending on who was asked.

Another homicide investigator who responded was Detective Bob Kenney. Garrulous and quick-witted, Kenney was beloved by almost everyone on the job. He was the thoughtful one, the one who could pore over a case file and find something that had been overlooked. He had also garnered the support of a number of law enforcement officials across Massachusetts—even the Massachusetts State Police, who historically shared a fractious relationship with municipal police forces, had a special affection for Kenney.

Kenney had taken on a notoriously crooked state senator and won. Her name was Dianne Wilkerson. On the day that Julissa Brisman was murdered the senator had earned the dubious moniker the "Boston Bra Stuffer" or "Senator Sleazy" because of the federal indictment that had been leveled against her. The federal charges of accepting bribes were accompanied by very damaging photographs taken by an undercover FBI agent of the senator stuffing hundred-dollar bills into her bra at a posh eatery in the shadow of Boston's State House. She and Kenney had become adversaries during the trial of her nephew, Jermaine Berry, who had been charged with murdering a young Navy sailor in a bar fight years earlier. In an attempt to win an appeal for Berry, his powerful politician aunt testified that Detective Bob Kenney lied about a confession her nephew gave in the case. She accused Kenney of manipulating witness statements that were taped in the case, saying that the detective had turned off the recording when information that could have exonerated her nephew was given.

Weeks before the cops would converge in the twentieth floor hallway of the Marriot Copley the FBI would charge that Wilkerson had in fact lied in her nephew's case. The tape had never been turned off, forensic experts at the FBI headquarters in Quantico had determined. The feds were not going to deal with this woman lightly anymore. She had been in trouble before, certainly. But United States Attorney Michael Sullivan had had enough of the shenanigans of the Massachusetts State House. Three—three—Speakers of the House of Representatives found themselves on the ugly end of a federal indictment. Three in a row. The first was Charlie Flaherty, who had earned the moniker "Good Time Charlie" by a local columnist for the Boston *Herald*. Flaherty's speakership collapsed in 1996 after he agreed to plead guilty to federal income tax evasion and pay a combined $50,000 in state and federal fines following a two-and-a-half-year investigation into his relationship with lobbyists, also precipitated by a series of stories in the *Globe*.

Staggeringly, Flaherty is now a registered lobbyist on Beacon Hill.

After Flaherty a rough-and-tumble Dorchester guy named Tom Finneran was locked up by the feds and later convicted of lying to a federal agent. Finneran stepped down before he was indicted in June 2005 for obstruction of justice and perjury in connection with a civil suit filed in federal court challenging a legislative redistricting plan. He was playing games with the ways in which votes would be counted in Boston's historically segregated neighborhoods. In a plea deal with federal prosecutors in January 2007, Finneran admitted he obstructed justice, received 18 months of unsupervised probation, and a $25,000 fine, and the perjury counts were dismissed. Not surprisingly, Finneran did not take that serious of a hit. Finneran now makes a healthy six-figure salary hosting a talk radio program.

And right after Senator Dianne Wilkerson, along with her friend City Councilor Chuck Turner, were charged with taking bribes as part of an undercover FBI sting, Finneran's successor as the Speaker of the House also stepped down. Sal DiMasi was probably one of the most powerful men in Massachusetts. Garrulous and popular in the last neighborhood that saw a Mafia stronghold in Boston, the North End, DiMasi is suspected of using his position to funnel a lucrative software contract to his business partner. His trial is expected to come this year. He has resigned from office. Then at the start of 2010 another state senator, Anthony Galluccio, was sent to jail after he got into a hit-and-run accident—not his first. The crash took place fourteen hours after Cambridge police gave him a ride home after finding him legless in a gas station parking lot. He had thrown an open bar fundraiser for his reelection campaign and apparently partook in more than his fair share of the free booze. A judge had sentenced him to house arrest and ordered him to stay off the bottle. He didn't. But worse, he blamed his failed breathalyzer test on "over-active oral hygiene." The mouthwash defense didn't work and Galluccio was sentenced to a year behind bars.

Massachusetts politics are a very nasty business indeed. The last thing any cop in Boston wants is to get in that pig sty and roll around with the swine. But Bob Kenney was not going to let anyone call him a liar. And he was not going to let Jermaine Berry get away with murder—even if his aunt was a longtime and very powerful senator. Wilkerson, who made no secret of her disdain for the BPD, was going down. And the people who mattered in the black community, the ministers and the street workers and fellow cops, had to accept that Bob Kenney had done everything by the book in the Jermaine Berry murder case now that the feds had Dianne Wilkerson in their sights.

As a result, every time Bob Kenney showed up at a crime scene, other cops wanted to shake his hand. That night was a bit different though. The congratulations he received were muted by the horrific crime that the officers had to begin to break down. That night there was a hush even among the most seasoned, calloused investigators as they began the task of trying to rebuild the moments leading up to the discovery of the petite brunette who sucked in her last breaths with her feet in her hotel room and her head in the hallway.

It did not take long to piece together what likely went down that night between the scantily-clad woman and her killer. Surveillance photos showed a tall blond man coming up an escalator toward an elevator bank at 10:06 p.m. His demeanor was nearly identical to the way he strolled out of the Westin Hotel four days earlier. His head was lowered over his BlackBerry as he text-messaged someone, maybe even his "date," telling her he had arrived as he walked in. He was wearing the same black coat, only this time his face was fully visible. He was wearing dress slacks and a collared polo shirt. He left the hotel with that same nonchalance. He didn't have a worry in the world.

He must have immediately pulled out the plastic zip-ties as she opened the door; the same type of restraints he used to bind Trisha Leffler four nights earlier. But he only managed to secure one tie on Julissa's wrists before the five-foot-five woman began to struggle. She only weighed 105 pounds but she must have put up a hell of a fight. After all, she was brought up on the hardscrabble streets of New York City. She was a woman who once declared on her MySpace page, "I am a true born and raised Manhattan hottie." No way in hell was she going to let some frat boy get the best of her if she could help it. It wasn't in her nature to give up in a fight. But this was one fight she couldn't win.

She was bashed in the head with the butt end of a gun. The blows came one after another, hits so sharp and violent that her skull was fractured in several places, the medical examiner would later determine. She still fought back, scratching her attacker. He responded with ferocity, maybe even fear, but ultimately deadly force.

There were three shots with what investigators would later learn was a 9mm semi-automatic pistol. One hit her chest and passed through her back. A second bullet hit her in the stomach and the third shot ripped into her heart. She was still in her panties and bra when she fell. A piece of the plastic tie was still fastened to her wrist when the security guard found her halfway in, halfway out of her room on the twentieth floor. Her other wrist was bruised and welted.

A few minutes after the cops arrived at the Marriott Copley Place crime scene, word got back to the detectives leading the investigation into the Trisha Leffler case that there had been another similar robbery at another posh hotel just down the street. But it wasn't just another robbery, it was now also a homicide. Ten days shy of her twenty-sixth birthday, Julissa Brisman was pronounced dead at 10:36 p.m., shortly after arriving at Boston Medical Center.

The hospital would turn out to be the same place where Phil Markoff the medical student was slated to begin an internship. He had already visited the ER as a student. He may have even been in the same bay where doctors desperately tried to save the young woman's life before finally pronouncing her dead.

Her murder would set off a massive manhunt and media shitstorm that would only escalate even further when word got out that Julissa died in the very emergency room where her accused killer planned to undertake a medical residency. Boston Medical Center boasted one of the best trauma emergency rooms in the country. It was the place where cops went when they were shot. Every city has that kind of superb trauma center and the old BMC (which is what cops and doctors and locals still called the hospital) was that spot for New England. Sure, Massachusetts General Hospital had the international reputation. But if you were a bleeder—had a gunshot wound or were stabbed—reputations didn't matter, you wanted transport to BMC.

Mary Beth Simons never got that text message

that she had been expecting, alerting her that the transaction with "Andy" had been completed and that Julissa was safe. She texted Brisman three times, around 11 p.m., at midnight and then again at 5:30 a.m. before her anxiety that kept her up all night became too much. The next morning she called security at the Marriot Copley hotel and was immediately transferred to an investigator at the Boston Police Department. Simons was a smart woman. After the initial shock of learning Julissa was dead she knew her computer records could help track the client who was likely responsible—"Andy."

It was 7:10 a.m., investigators would note, when Simons called with the clues that would help detectives track down the killer: his email address, AM DPM@Live.com, and the cell phone number he had used to call Mary Beth to confirm his appointment.

One thing that investigators noted immediately was that there was a clear sign of a struggle. One of Julissa's nails had broken in the struggle, which meant she might have raked her hands across the killer's skin. In a cop's world that was good news in an otherwise horrifying situation. This woman was young and pretty. She was killed in a high-profile location. It was bound to be a media circus. And not just a local media circus: In this case the BPD detectives would also have to put up with the notorious New York press. To the investigators working the case that meant the BPD brass would be up their asses every minute of every day that there wasn't an arrest in

the case. Until someone was wearing the silver bracelets, the BPD detectives could count on there being
no time with their kids or wives, no days off, no
working on other cases, nothing but Julissa Brisman 24/7.

Another report was written up:

> "About 10:13 p.m. on Tuesday April 14, 2009
> Officer [John] Turcotte assigned to the D435F
> unit responded to 110 Huntington Avenue (Co-
> pley Marriott Hotel) for an unconscious female
> on the 20th floor. Boston Fire Department En-
> gine 33 arrived at the same time. Upon arrival
> security updated police and fire regarding the
> unconscious female possibly being the victim
> of an assault where she was stabbed and that
> hotel security could not find her pulse. Officer
> Turcotte and Boston Fire upon arrive to room
> 2034 observed the female victim laying un-
> responsive. BFD started CPR until relieved by
> Boston EMS and transported to Boston Medi-
> cal center."

Then those awful words: "Full notification requested."

Someone had to do the awful job of finding the
people who loved Julissa Brisman and tell them that
she was dead.

The report included a litany of responding agencies and units from the Boston Police Department.

There was a whack job on the loose, someone who struck two hotels in four days on the same upscale street in the nicest part of Boston.

It was easy to understand why hotel security guards thought that Brisman had been stabbed to death. There was so much blood it was hard to discern the bullet holes in her body. Her head was so swollen. It was really hard to imagine that the macabre scene had played out in a matter of minutes in a crowded hotel at a time that the restaurants underneath the hotel were packed with people taking in Boston's sights.

The following day another report was written up:

"On Wednesday April 15, 2009 Doctor Mindy Hull of the Office of the Chief Medical Examiner performed an autopsy on the body of Julissa Brisman and determined the cause of death to be a gunshot wound and the manner of death a homicide. On this same date about 17:00 hours Detective Kenney and James Freeman . . . and other officers of the Homicide Unit met with family members of Julissa Brisman at the Office of the Chief Medical Examiner and were present when they identified the deceased as Julissa Brisman. Incident to be upgraded to a homicide."

No one was surprised that the medical examiner ruled the death of Julissa Brisman a homicide. The poor girl was a bloodied mess. And she clearly left some damage on the body of her attacker. Homicide investigators knew that the scratches would be yet another tool they could use as a surefire way to identify the assailant. They had his DNA.

Now all the BPD had to do was find a guy with the corresponding scratches on his skin.

7

The police might have been expecting a media flood; what they got instead was a tsunami. The out-of-town media converged en masse in Boston less than twelve hours after Brisman had been killed. There's nothing like the murder of a pretty young woman, especially one who could be splashed across the front page dressed only in lingerie or a bathing suit, to get an editor's interest and make a story extra "newsworthy." It's even juicier when that newsworthy event takes place in one of the toniest neighborhoods in the country, the Back Bay of Boston.

Suffolk County district attorney Dan Conley and Boston police commissioner Edward Davis needed to release a statement—feed the media beast, as they say. Some reporters had already spoken to police sources and they knew that there had been a similar attack on a woman who had advertised on Craigslist—just as Julissa Brisman had. Much to Davis and Conley's chagrin, by Thursday afternoon, April 15, the crime had earned the tabloid moniker of "The Craigslist Killer."

The Boston Regional Intelligence Center, a command post at police headquarters in the Roxbury section of Boston, had compiled enough information to keep the rabid reporters who were being harassed by harried editors at bay. The release read:

IDENTIFICATION WANTED
Death Investigation at Copley-Marriott Hotel
Wednesday, April 15, 2009
The following information was released by
the Boston Police Department via the BPD
News website (http://bpdnews.com)
on 4/15/2009.

On Tuesday April 14, 2009, at approximately 10:13pm, officers from District 4 responded to a report of an unconscious female at the Copley Marriott Hotel at 110 Huntington Ave. Upon arrival, hotel security updated the police that the unconscious female may have been the victim of an assault, possibly a stabbing. Officers observed the 26 year-old [sic] white female victim suffering from what was determined to be multiple gunshot wounds to the torso. The preliminary investigation suggests that the victim was advertising masseuse services on Craigslist. Detectives are investigating the possibility that this incident was an attempted robbery. It appears that the victim engaged in a struggle in the threshold of the hotel room immediately prior to the shooting.

Detectives are currently investigating the possibility that this incident is related to another recent incident which also occurred at a local hotel recently.

On April 10, 2009, at approximately 12:46am, officers responded to a robbery in progress at the Westin Hotel at 10 Huntington Ave. Officers received a report from a 29 year old female victim that she was robbed at gunpoint in her hotel room.

The Boston Police Homicide Unit is actively investigating the facts and circumstances of this incident and urges anyone with information regarding this incident to notify them by calling (617) 343-4470. Individuals wishing to provide information anonymously may do so by calling the Crime Stoppers Tip Line at 1-800-494-TIPS or texting 'TIP' to CRIME (27463). The Boston Police strictly protects the identity of all individuals wishing to provide information anonymously.

The release was accompanied by photographs of the tall blond man taken by surveillance cameras at the Westin Copley Place hotel on April 10 and then from the Marriot Copley Place hotel minutes after the murder. And it came with an almost laughable, cover-your-ass disclaimer: "This individual is NOT wanted at this time. This information is being provided for identification and questioning purposes only. Independent and corroborating information should be obtained before any actions are taken."

Right, the Boston police commissioner and district attorney were releasing pictures of a man to the press, which was ready to send them all over the world, who was "NOT wanted at this time." Just some schmoe they wanted to interview? Not likely. Dan Conley then read a similar statement for the assembled cameras about the man who was ostensibly "NOT wanted."

"On Tuesday April 14, 2009, at approximately 10:13 p.m., officers from District 4 responded to a report of an unconscious female at the Copley Marriott Hotel [sic] at 110 Huntington Ave. Upon arrival, hotel security updated the police that the unconscious female may have been the victim of an assault, possibly a stabbing. Officers observed Ms. Brisman suffering from what was determined to be multiple gunshot wounds to the torso," Conley stated.

Conley was a lifelong politician. The reporters who exclusively covered courts and cops were not only interested in what Conley had to say about the murder but they were also closely monitoring the body language between Conley and Davis. The two men had gotten into a very public spat months earlier and that tiff had not ended yet.

Ordinarily, Boston police homicide investigators investigated murders within the city of Boston. However, Conley had declared that the Massachusetts State Police would be the lead investigative agency for slayings in public parks and on MBTA buses, which were technically state property. There were a lot of murders on MBTA buses and since 2000 Boston police had solved six, leaving just one case open. It was a slap in the face to the BPD, who were already sensitive to criticism about their low murder and arrest rates. Conley's backing the state troopers over the BPD created unnecessary tension, a turf war, between the "staties," as Bostonians called them, and the BPD. Some say that the usually measured Davis retaliated by replacing the head of the homicide division, a guy from the close-knit Boston neighborhood of Charlestown named Dan Coleman who happened to be drinking buddies and good friends with Conley.

Coleman had a lot of juice in Boston neighborhoods, especially Irish strongholds like Dorchester, South Boston and Charlestown, areas in which its residents actually showed up at polling locations. Other neighborhoods were more likely to be home to recent immigrants, many of whom were trying to stay out of the watchful eye of city officials. They sure as hell weren't going to show up to vote for them. Coleman's sway and sprawling family roots in those powerful Irish neighborhoods led to a lot of political donations to his friend Conley's campaign coffers. The district attorney was furious that "his guy" had been bumped from the helm of the homicide division. And Davis, an outsider brought in from Lowell to shake up the BPD, frankly didn't give a shit. He had a department to run. Coleman wasn't pulling his weight, he told people.

Covering crime in Boston often overlapped into politics. Sometimes it was the same beat: crime and politics were one and the same, reporters often joked. And in Massachusetts some of the most corrupt criminals happened to have been voted into the buildings that they stole from by their friends and neighbors. In return those friends and neighbors received "hack jobs" or patronage appointments. It was an unrelenting cycle. There were so many hacks that the same pols got elected over and over again.

The press conference about the murder at the Marriott Copley was one of the rare occasions when the district attorney and police commissioner were standing side-by-side in recent months.

But on that day they had a common goal. They needed this killer caught. They wanted to make sure there were no other victims than Julissa and Trisha Leffler, wanted to be sure that the so-called "Craigslist Killer" was a media invention and not the next Son of Sam. Davis was no dummy. He had been briefed on Leffler's statements and was fully aware that the street-smart hooker had even remarked that it seemed her attacker "had done it before." They wanted anyone with information to come forward because no matter how much cops bitch about reporters, getting photos shown on the media was how killers and rapists and robbers got caught. Someone might recognize this guy. Usually security photos were useless. The perp knew enough to look away from the cameras or the equipment was so old the images were about as recognizable as the images on a wet newspaper. But not this guy. He strolled in and out of both hotels like he didn't have a care in the world. They actually had a shot of using these pictures to garner some helpful tips on the identity of the tall blond preppie who walked in and out of the hotels.

Politics would have to take a back seat to crime fighting. For now, they needed to present a united front. Davis and Conley stood shoulder to shoulder, or Davis's shoulder to the top of Conley's head, on that afternoon readying to feed the media beast yet again. Reporters could not help but wonder if one of the reasons that Conley hated the police commissioner is that Davis just made him painfully aware of how difficult his slight stature was going to make it for him to ever achieve his political aspirations. Dan Conley, a former prosecutor and Boston City Councilor, had dreams of being the mayor of Boston one day. It sure as hell wasn't going to happen when the loveable "Mumbles" Menino was still around. And it wasn't going to happen if Bostonians, who demanded a certain New England salty swagger, saw him as a little bitter guy who couldn't hold his own.

Conley hated being photographed next to Davis and most of the reporters standing in front of him knew it all too well.

But none of that would even be up for discussion unless they caught the Craigslist Killer. Because if the Craigslist Killer wasn't caught, Conley wouldn't be able to get elected dog catcher, let alone mayor, in Boston.

But at least for now, Conley was the top dog. He was going to be the "talking head," as reporters referred to the people who would provide the sound, the one that would take the mike.

Conley urged anyone with information to call the police. Davis praised the work of his cops. The BRIC (Boston Regional Intelligence center) was already abuzz with activity. Mary Beth Simons began to cooperate with police, providing investigators with every email exchanged with "Andy."

They had an email address—AMDPM@Live .com—and with that the subscriber's personal information was just a subpoena away.

8

Philip Markoff was not a high roller. No one from Foxwoods was going to send a chartered plane to pick him up. That was something Foxwoods only did for big shots like Nick Varano, a Boston restaurateur who was written up in magazines across the country, or for his friends and fellow high stakes gamblers, businessmen like David Modica who owned an eatery in the neighborhood of East Boston called Ecco. Primarily Boston guys with connections and cash or Rhode Island gangsters (and there were plenty of those). Those guys could pick up the phone, call their "liaison" and be on a jet within an hour or so. Those guys got first-class treatment in terms of MGM suites, choice dining reservations at the upscale restaurant Paragon and "comped" tickets to whatever entertainment they felt like seeing, be it the Bon Jovi reunion tour or Chris Rock's sold-out comedy act. There was even a private penthouse casino for those guys. They were the real deal. They

were the high rollers. They were the guys with political clout back in Boston and the bank to back up
their bets.

Markoff wasn't a high roller but he also wasn't
Foxwoods' lowest-level customer either, a day-tripper
who climbed off a $20 round-trip bus to blow his
paycheck or a retiree who spent the afternoon feed-
ing the slots. He was a mid-level gambler. A regular. He was cultivated by casino management for
one reason—loyalty. If they treated players like
Markoff—who traveled to Foxwoods with increasing frequency—like a bigger shot than he really was,
he would be less likely to drive to their competition,
the Mohegan Sun casino. With the economy in the
dumper, Foxwoods, which survived on razor-thin
operating margins, needed all the cash flow it could
get it hands on, meaning it needed as many Philip
Markoffs cramming their poker and blackjack tables as possible. That's why Markoff was instantly
approved for a Wampum Rewards Card, which acts
basically like a prepaid credit card and can be swiped
at ATM-like machines at the slot machines and
gaming tables. He was assigned a patron number,
05126939, and a rank, 6D. In Foxwoods' rating system, 6D is considered middle class. Even his birthday was logged: February 12, 1986. So was his New
York driver's license number. Times were getting
tight, though. Markoff had applied for a credit limit
which would allow him to access cash advances. He
gave his mother's address in Sherrill, the tiny little

town in upstate New York, for all correspondence. Foxwoods understood. They were sticklers about getting paid; not so much about where guys who frequented the casino wanted any correspondence to be sent.

Markoff made it clear that he did not want to receive any mail from the casino; didn't want his wife-to-be to know the extent of his habit. Of course, Megan knew that he liked to gamble. They had discussed honeymooning at a casino, after all. But Philip did not want his fiancée to know that he was popping down to Foxwoods as often as he was, a couple of times a month or more these days, spending money that he should have been socking away for their future.

As Megan became more wrapped up in planning the wedding, returning more frequently to New Jersey to hash out the details of the big day with her mother, Philip was able to go to Foxwoods more often. He was there April 2 and it was a good day . . . for the casino. Pulling four $100 bills out of his jeans pockets, he played poker for $75 a hand. He lost all of it. He moved on to a blackjack table and pulled out the remaining $400 he had in his pocket, cashing it in for four $100 chips. Four hands, four black chips, four hundred dollars lost. It took only a couple of minutes. Maybe that's what the old Foxwoods jingle meant by *"The wonder of it all."* I wonder what the hell happened to all that money in less than five minutes. In no time, Philip had lost the equivalent of more than half their rent money. Undeterred, he pressed on only to more than double his losses that day, a total of $1,650 all told.

Ten days later, Markoff was back. On April 12—two days after a prostitute named Trisha Leffler was robbed by a man who bore a striking resemblance to the medical student—Markoff lost $550 at the blackjack table. If you added in the losses he sustained on a previous March 28 trip to Foxwoods, Markoff had lost more than $3,400 in about two weeks. Maybe a highly paid Boston doctor could afford that kind of scratch, but not a struggling medical student like Markoff. Good thing it wasn't all his money he was blowing. Probably none of it was, which was exactly why Boston detectives thought he had other marks. The $800 police believe he took from Trisha Leffler was a pittance. It remained unclear if had been was able to grab any cash off the dead woman, Julissa Brisman. He has not been charged with robbery in that case. But less than forty-eight hours after he'd fled the Boston Marriott where Brisman was found, Markoff was already playing again. Of course, he had to take pains to cover the scratches on his body as he sat at the blackjack table. He didn't need any strangers noticing him. And luckily the cameras over his head did not discern the scratches. His fiancée Megan would not even notice them. She wouldn't be home for two days. By then the welts could be easily explained: a neighbor's cat. Aggressive shower scrubbing. She

was so focused on the wedding he could tell her anything.

Meanwhile, police were working furiously to deci-
pher the true identity of Julissa Brisman's last client,
"Andy." As the cops worked around the clock on the
case, the slain woman's friends were inundated with
phone calls from reporters from across the country.
The story was tabloid heaven. Tawdry sexual ads on
the Internet, a gorgeous young victim, plenty of available eye-popping photographs of her wearing nothing other than lingerie or bathing suits. And to top it
all off, the suspect wasn't some run-of-the-mill street
thug but someone who looked like so many of the
college students who flocked to Boston each year: a
young white guy wearing a baseball cap, jeans and
zip-up jacket, incessantly using his BlackBerry.

As the newspapers and TV newscast went ba-
nanas with the story, police detectives undertook
the grim task of breaking the news of Julissa Brisman's death to her mother, Carmen Guzman.

After the detectives left and Guzman had cried
herself out, she began calling her daughter's friends.
She didn't know what else to do. It made absolutely
no sense what the police had just told her. Her daughter was giving sensual massages for money? One of
her "clients" killed her during a violent struggle?
In Boston? Was it the man she had met on the train?
Who?

The mother and daughter had been close. Guzman
had shared in her daughter's struggle with alcohol

and drugs and her efforts to stay sober. They bonded over it, in fact.

In early May 2008, Brisman asked her mother what she wanted for the upcoming Mother's Day. "She said, 'I already got the best Mother's Day present you could ever give me, your sobriety,'" Julissa wrote in her diary. "(It) put a smile on my face. I know, cheesy, but being sober makes me smile."

Being a sensual masseuse specializing in "hand stress release," however, was not something that Julissa shared with her mother.

Carmen Guzman did not speak a lot of English. She was from the Dominican Republic, where she had been a doctor. But she could never pass the necessary tests in the United States to continue her career. And even though she had lived in New York for the past quarter century, she never really mastered the language. In New York, you didn't need to speak English. There were so many Spanish speakers she could easily get by with just her native tongue and a few words of English or Spanglish, as some called it. But on that terrible morning after her daughter was murdered, she spoke two English words she had hoped never to have to utter.

"Julissa died," she whispered to her daughter's friends. And then she would weep.

"Julissa died."

The day after her daughter was found slain, Carmen Guzman and other members of her family were brought to Boston Police Department headquarters at

One Schroeder Plaza, a building named after two BPD brothers, Walter and John, who were killed in the line of duty within three years of each other in the early 1970s. Walter was shot dead by the domestic terrorist network Weather Underground. (Walter Schroeder's murder would become an integral part of the Obama campaign in 2008 because of the presidential contender's relationship with Weather Underground founder Bill Ayers. Bostonians, especially cops, were bitter about Obama's connection to Ayers, who remained unrepentant about his bombing days and was quoted in the *New York Times* as saying, "I don't regret setting bombs. I wish I had done more," on September 11, 2001.) Walter's brother John was shot dead in an unrelated pawn shop robbery in the Boston neighborhood of Roxbury three years later as he investigated a home invasion. His killer would be released from jail in 2008 only to be rearrested in Rhode Island a month after his release.

Sergeant Detective Dan Keeler was at the meeting in One Schroeder Plaza that morning representing the robbery unit. So were Bobby Merner and Bob Kenney, the homicide investigators. The man in charge was Sergeant Detective Daniel Duff, and another key homicide investigator, Jimmy Freeman, was also asked to sit in. It was a very rough morning for everyone in the room, family and cops. Not only did Carmen Guzman have to hear graphic details about her daughter's murder and the shocking revelation of what she was doing in Boston in the first place, but she had to identify the bloody remains to make sure that the woman in the city's morgue at Boston City Hospital was, in fact, her daughter.

Even the most seasoned investigator hated this task. And that day it was Detective Bob Kenney who had the sad duty of watching a mother wail at the sight of her child rendered unrecognizable by bullets. Hair matted with blood. The child they had nurtured, their baby, ripped apart by bullets. It's a task that homicide detectives perform all too often but one they can't get used to: the crying, vomiting, uncontrollable shakes, fainting, sometimes even heart attacks. They have heard gut-wrenching screeches that subsequently haunted their dreams. Each parent reacts differently but the grief is usually the same, unrelenting. For the homicide detectives who have to accompany the loved ones to the morgue near Boston Medical Center in a building that had seen a spate of scandals in recent years, they are forced to watch another life destroyed—only the ones left behind die much more slowly. Mothers are the worst. The violence that has taken their child is just as savage on them. It is as if someone ages fifteen years in a single second, the pain hits them so hard. Each time the detectives know the person who is making the identification at a city morgue is now broken and damaged. Their own life expectancy takes a dip. Grief can do that to someone. It acts like a cancer. And with parents, grief is accompanied by guilt. *What could they have done better in raising their kid? What might have prevented this? Was it their fault?* The combination can physically alter the stature of a parent almost immediately. Cops see it in their stance, slumped shoulders, rounded backs, creased foreheads.

With Carmen Guzman it was no different. She screamed. Her sobs seemed like they would never stop.

Then she signed the paperwork that allowed a medical examiner to autopsy her daughter's remains. The findings were not surprising to investigators. The cause of death was determined to be a gunshot wound. The manner of death was a homicide.

For the detectives, they were fueled by the awful sound of a mother's cries. They were working on no sleep and their hearts pumped with too much caffeine. They were going to catch this yuppie scumbag and they were going to drag him into a courtroom in handcuffs. They were going to do that for Carmen Guzman. They were going to do that for Julissa.

To do that, the detectives needed the public's help, which meant they needed to reach out to the media, yet another task that made many detectives blanch. There were likely other victims, women who were afraid to come forward, which is what police believe Philip Markoff was counting on when he went to Brisman's room.

The first step was to release photographs of the suspect who had already earned the moniker "The Craigslist Killer," so dubbed by the *Boston Herald*, the go-to paper for crime buffs. Within hours, investigators took the security surveillance photos from the Westin Copley Place and the Marriott Copley hotels and cropped them to show the six-foot-three blond. His face was obscured in the photos taken at the Westin Copley where a prostitute named Trisha Leffler was left tied to the doorknob of her hotel room. In that photo, the baseball hat the suspect pulled down over his face shadowed his features. His head was bowed as he text-messaged someone.

The second picture, from the Marriot Copley, was much clearer. In fact, Leffler took one look at the photograph and exclaimed to the cops: "How did you get such a good picture of him?"

It was a promising start. They had a positive identification from a woman who had been in this guy's company for roughly fifteen minutes. She didn't hesitate for a second. Unlike Brisman, Trisha Leffler may not have put up a fight, but that was a good thing. She would become the key witness against her attacker in the coming days.

Meanwhile, the case was getting the "red ball" treatment; every available cop on the BPD was assigned to it, as many "boots on the ground" as possible. The Craigslist Killer Task Force was set up. Specialists assigned to the Boston Regional Intelligence Center (BRIC) were charged with sorting through the tips that poured in from the public, separating the nutty calls from the legitimate leads. The fugitive squad, led by Lieutenant Brian Albert, was brought in. Even the NYPD Cyber Crimes Squad assisted. It's somewhat out of the ordinary for the Boston Police Department to reach out to the New York Police Department, but the NYPD Cyber Crimes Squad was lauded across the nation as the best in the business at tracking fingerprints left in cyberspace. Together they joined forces with one shared goal: Find the Craigslist Killer. Find the man who had brutally killed a woman who only weighed 105 pounds. Reluctantly—because the BPD is notorious for keeping investigations close to the vest and out of the press—they turned to the media for help by releasing the cropped surveillance photos.

The date was April 16. Julissa Brisman had been dead for two days. It had been six days since Trisha Leffler had been bound and robbed of her money, her credit cards and her panties.

By the time the photographs of the Craigslist Killer were splashed all over the media, Markoff had driven south toward Connecticut and was gambling the days away in his safe place—Foxwoods.

But before he checked in on April 15, Markoff had business to attend to, a stop to make. He had money in his pocket and he wanted to play but it wasn't a big enough bankroll for the $75-per-hand poker game Markoff preferred playing. Megan was coming home in a few days and he needed to make the rent that he had lost days earlier during his last visit to Foxwoods. So Philip Markoff made another "date" through Craigslist. Her name was Cynthia

Melton. She was a 26-year-old stripper who was such a sensation at the Cadillac Lounge in Providence, Rhode Island, that one online reviewer called her the "reigning hot psycho bitch" at the club.

Markoff used one of his "dump phones"—a TracFone—that he purchased so no one could trace his calls or text messages. The appointment was set at the Holiday Inn Express in Warwick, a Rhode Island city of about 86,000 just south of Providence that advertises itself as being at "The Crossroads of New England," whatever that means. Markoff had found Melton's ads under the "Erotic Services" category of Craigslist among explicit listings such as:

"Good Girl Gone Bad."

"Ready Right Now."

"Cum and Play."

"I Only Look Like I'm Innocent."

"Bang U During Your Lunch Break."

"Lap Dances for Lotharios."

"Hot Young Mama Looking to Feel Good."

Melton, or "Amber" as she called herself, was a little less lascivious in her Craigslist ads, listing herself simply available for lap dances—$100.

Her phone rang around 9:30 at night. It was a man who wanted a date. He was calling from a "private" number. He asked her a price. She told him. He asked her location and room number, then said he'd text her when he was close.

The text message arrived at 10:51 p.m. She opened the door to a youngish-looking man wearing a brown baseball hat pulled close over his eyes. The security system at the Holiday Inn didn't get a good shot of his face but showed what he was wearing; blue jeans and a pink polo shirt with the same black jacket he wore for his "dates" with Julissa Brisman, aka "Morgan," and Trisha Leffler.

Cops would learn that he purchased the hat at a nearby Walmart at 10 p.m. By then, Markoff would have had to have known that it would be stupid to walk out of the Marriott Copley hotel without a hat on. Police believe he put the hat on in a lame attempt to hide his face. His picture had been all over the news all day long. He didn't want the stripper to recognize him before he got into the room. But Cynthia Melton wasn't exactly one to read the newspapers or watch the nightly TV newscasts. She had been busy turning tricks that day; her husband Keith had checked into the next room for safety reasons.

"I turned around and he had a gun," Melton would tell detectives. "His hands were shaking. The gun was black. He looked really nervous."

Still, despite the tremors, the gunman tried to gag her with a ball gag—the type used in the movie *Pulp Fiction* and very popular with the S&M set. She thrashed violently, knowing that her husband was waiting to hear from her that the client had arrived. They had a text message safety system worked out that actually worked. When that text would not come immediately, her husband knew there might be trouble.

She refused to acquiesce to the bondage tool but the man was deftly able to bind Cynthia Melton's hands with a zip-tie nevertheless.

Then her attacker tried to reassure her. He kept repeating the same thing over and over again as if he was trying to convince himself of something—not her.

"I'm not going to kill you. I'm not going to kill you. I don't want to kill you. I just need money.

"I don't want to kill you. Don't worry. I'm just broke. I need some cash or some cards."

As he rifled through her belongings, there was a knock on the door. The assailant—who once again neglected to put on gloves as he rifled through the exotic dancer's hotel room—spun around and pointed the gun at Cynthia Melton.

"Who is that?!" he screamed.

Before Melton could answer, her husband used an extra key he had for his wife's room and entered. The gunman pointed the weapon at Keith Melton, who slowly backed out of the room, refusing to turn around. As he walked backward he lost his footing and fell.

The robber ran out the door and down three flights of stairs and was gone. Cynthia and her husband called the police. They had nothing to fear. Prostitution behind closed doors is legal in Rhode Island so they would not face any criminal charges for the lap-dance business they were running out of the hotel.

In the end, Markoff left empty-handed. He drove

back to the place where he felt he could hide among the masses—Foxwoods.

He sat down at a blackjack table and began to play again.

And he walked away from the table with $5,300. His luck had finally changed, or so he thought.

9

Boston detectives were astonished when they received the call that the so-called Craigslist Killer
had struck again, for the third time in a week.

"He's a brazen prick, huh," one of the detectives
said to another while hanging up the phone. "His
picture is all over the news."

Rhode Island Attorney General Patrick Lynch's
office was immediately inundated with phone calls.
Reporters covering the story had a new hot lead, a
new locale, another twist in the "Craigslist Killer
case." Like this story didn't have "legs" enough already. The reporters were excited to be on the move
again, happy to be anywhere but camped out at Boston police headquarters waiting for the few crumbs
of new information that the police commissioner
and district attorney dropped at their daily press
conferences.

The story for now was an hour south. At the very
least they would be able to get "sound," meaning that

Lynch would actually do what is dubbed in the media business as a "show and tell." Essentially, that meant that Lynch would read his press release into a bank of microphones so that the news stations would have something to lead with, but he wouldn't answer any questions. After all, this wasn't Lynch's case/head-ache by a long shot. All they had in Warwick was an attempted robbery, not a high-profile murder. And the victim was uncooperative, which was a night-mare for Rhode Island cops. Through a spokesman Lynch would only say that Warwick police have de-veloped "promising information" about the April 16 robbery at the Holiday Inn Express & Suites. "Al-though we're encouraged by the progress being made, this is a complex investigation and is going to take more time," he said.

It took a couple more days but by April 18 Boston police finally came up with a name to go with the surveillance photos of the suspected Craigslist Killer. Given the appearance of the perpetrator, the police would not by then have been surprised if the killer turned out to be a yuppie or even possibly a college student. But any detective who would later claimed they had an inkling all along that the suspect was a *medical student* was flat-out lying. At the very least some of the mistakes made in the room would indi-cate that the attacker made some pretty dumb errors: putting the gloves on after he bound and gagged Leffler, walking right by the surveillance cameras. Those rookie moves were certainly would not seem to be the actions of a guy intelligent enough to earn himself a spot into one of the country's best medical schools.

On April 18, 2009, the Boston police had an announcement to make: "Currently Boston Police detectives do believe, based upon a number of similarities, that there is a strong connection between the Warwick incident, the homicide at the Copley Marriott, and the armed robbery at the Westin Hotel. Boston Police continue to work closely with the Warwick Police. In addition, Boston Police investigators are aggressively following up on all information received from the community. There are no additional images or information available to be released at this time. Boston Police Media Relations will continue to provide updates as appropriate."

What the Boston police officials didn't say that night—as Philip Markoff was finally beating the house at Foxwoods—was that the cyber sleuths had finally come up with an identity for the suspect they had been hunting for the past eight days.

The Craigslist Killer went to some lengths to try to hide his identity when contacting his victims through the Internet. But unlike the disposable Trac-Fones that police believe Markoff employed specifically to cover up his tracks, the Internet almost always leaves a cyber trail. "High tech fingerprints" would soon become the media buzz word.

Markoff had set up an email account with a server that was based in Redmond, Washington, called

Live.com. The server was a company owned by Microsoft Windows, which announced in the fall of 2008 that they expected to grow Live.com into the next Facebook or MySpace. (It never happened. In fact, if one tries to log onto Live.com these days one gets redirected to Bing.com.) Like any email server, it's easy enough to give them a fake name and address and other identifying information. That is what authorities claim Philip Markoff did.

But every computer connected to the Internet is assigned a unique number called an Internet Protocol (IP) address. Those numbers are recorded by the Internet server. Usually the numbers are private. But police can obtain those numbers via subpoenas.

Through the emails "Andy" sent, the police obtained his IP address and by subpoenaing Live.com they were able to determine that the emails were sent from a computer inside the building where Markoff lived with his fiancée. However, since Markoff had a wireless Internet connection it was possible that someone else in the building could have been sharing his Internet server. So the cops took up position outside the building and waited for a tall, handsome, young blond guy to arrive.

Sergeant Brian Albert from the fugitive task force and a handful of his cops were staked out outside Markoff's building at 8 Highpoint Circle in Quincy. It was certainly not a luxury building and there was nothing upscale about the neighborhood. The building had a common pool and a tennis court and there was a buzzer system. But other than those amenities, it was a run-of-the-mill suburban apartment complex.

It was Saturday evening, April 18. Six unmarked police cars in total circled the building, making sure they had an eye on the parking garage. Inside those cars were some of the most hardscrabble cops on the job, ones that were used to dangerous psychopaths and criminals on the lam. It promised to be a long night. As he waited, Sergeant Albert pored over the case file that had been compiled on his target—Philip Markoff.

Markoff was a twenty-three-year-old second-year medical student, part of Boston University Medical School's class of 2011. Most of his classes were held in Boston's South End at 72 Concord Street. He had a decent record. Boston University would not divulge his grades—not even to homicide investigators—but they would go as far to say that he was a very good student in good standing. No disciplinary history to speak of. Boston University Police had been briefed on the case and helped compile a photo array of pictures—including Markoff's student identification—to show the witness, Trisha Leffler. The student identification was also emailed to the Warwick Police Department. Both the lap dancer from Vegas who had been bound and robbed on April 10 at the Westin Copley hotel and the exotic dancer from Rhode Island who had been bound and robbed at the Holiday Inn in Warwick took one look at the picture and exclaimed: "That's him."

It was surprising news for most of Markoff's professors and his fellow students. Yet there was one woman who was not all that surprised to learn that Philip Markoff had a dark side. She had suspected it all along. As Markoff's lab partner, Tiffany Montgomery observed him day in, day out. Something about him creeped her out. "Disturbing," was the word she used to describe him. Montgomery told reporters that her lab partner suffered such dark mood swings that she contemplated telling school counselors that he might be suicidal. Other times, he'd come in and was as happy as a lark. He was either upbeat or comatose.

"He just wasn't right in the head, and I knew it, and probably other people did, too," said Montgomery, who spent hours with him each day in the lab.

"My friends from the lab group have confirmed that 'you weren't the only one feeling that way,'" she told the *Boston Globe*. "I got the impression he was really disturbed."

When reporters caught up to Montgomery, who had dropped out of medical school because of financial problems, she said Markoff's mood swings alarmed her.

"One day, he'd be warm and friendly and smiling," said Montgomery, who now works as a biotech consultant in Boston. "And the next day you'd see him and the clouds had rolled in. And you'd say to yourself, 'This is the 50 percent of the week when it's the upset, brooding Phil, and not the smiling happy Phil.' "

In addition to possibly connecting him to separate murder and kidnapping/robbery cases, the search of Markoff's email account also turned up some unexpected browsing that the future doctor had been up to on-line.

Found on Markoff's computer was a picture he apparently posted of his torso and hands wrapped around his erect penis on an alternative lifestyle website called Alt.com. Alt.com is a pay-per-month website that bills itself as "Your online adult personals, BDSM, Leather & Fetish Community." The site also posts erotic S&M pictures with headlines such as "The Tighter the Better," "I Love It When A Man Begs For Mercy" and "Yes It Hurt And It Was Worth It." Under "Looking for . . ." the site offers no less than 90 different types of fetishes.

Markoff clicked on the category of "transvestitism."

Calling himself sexaddict53885 he began to describe his preference as "submissive" and his experience level as "I am new at this." For a first-timer, police thought, he sure was able to supply a lot of kinky specifics.

"I am currently a graduate student looking to experiment with the BDSM [bondage, domination and sadomasochism] lifestyle. . . . I am very interested in being dominated and being made to do different things. Among those different things: anal sex. Being forced to wear a collar and leash, and cross dressing," he wrote.

"I am looking for anyone open minded; try new fetishes or show me what you know. I enjoy women . . . but I really want to meet a ts/tv/tg (transsexual, transvestite, transgender) for friendship and experimentation. I am looking for doms and switch's [sic] but I am open to experimenting with subs."

Despite the lengths sexaddict53885 used to hide his identity he used his real birthday, February 12, 1986, his real description, Blond, blue eyes, six-foot-three, and basically the place where he lived, Boston, Massachusetts.

He set up that profile in May of 2007, shortly after graduating from SUNY Albany. By then, he was in a serious relationship with Megan McAllister. Megan had no idea that her boyfriend may have had fantasies of dressing up in women's clothing and having sex with strangers who were transvestites or transgendered or transsexuals. Their relationship was of a more romantic nature. She had been in a terrible car crash that left her with lingering back problems and pain. They had an active sex life but it was unlikely that the couple engaged in the types of sexual experimentation that sexaddict53885 was looking for.

On April 20, after the police had spent almost two days "sitting" on the Highpoint Circle apartment building, Philip Markoff finally emerged from the building carrying luggage with an attractive blonde woman at his side.

"I was surprised at how much he looked like the pictures I saw from the incidents in Boston and Rhode Island," Albert would later say.

Undercover investigators tailed the couple all day as they went food shopping. Megan McAllister acted like the blushing bride-to-be that she was. Holding hands, affectionate, completely oblivious to Philip's dark side or the fact that he was being tailed by a dozen of Boston's finest because of it. Even the police would note that she was clearly much more enthralled with him than he seemed to be with her. But maybe that's because he had other things on his mind.

Albert radioed back to Police Commissioner Ed Davis personally. "I like this guy. It's him."

10

Police Commissioner Edward F. Davis III is different from most of Boston's past top cops. And not just because he's six feet, six inches tall.

Ed Davis's father had been a patrol officer in the hardscrabble Massachusetts town of Lowell and Davis had come up through the ranks of that small police department, advancing without political pull, which can be done in the towns outside of the Hub. But in Boston to become the police commissioner one usually has to be heavily politically connected. Many consider the Boston political scene to still be the quintessential old boys' network. Plum jobs like being named "PC" are bequeathed by the mayor (or whichever clique of city councilors he's indebted to) with long strings attached. In the fall of 2006, it stood to reason that the next police commissioner would have a "rabbi." "A rabbi" is cop slang for someone who watches out, a mentor who can make sure someone is taken care of on the job. Of course the "rabbi" also makes a few demands of his or her own. When you take care of someone it should come back in the form of undying loyalty within the Boston political network he or she would be beholden to. After all, Mayor Thomas Menino had gone out-of-network with his previous selection for top cop and that ended disastrously.

Sure, Kathleen O'Toole was as Irish as Paddy's pig, seemingly a pre-requisite for the Boston job, but some would later accuse Menino of playing the "PC" card, as in political correctness, by choosing a woman PC, the first woman PC in the history of the department at that. And many would view O'Toole's time heading the BPD as an abysmal failure.

Whether there was validity to the claim or it was just the usual macho cop bullshit, the rap within the BPD on O'Toole was that she wasn't a street cop, was never out at crime scenes, didn't like to go into the tough neighborhoods at all. She wasn't one of them. She was good at the ceremonial stuff, accepting awards at luncheons, flapping her gums about all the changes she was going to make at the BPD. A bureaucrat, for sure, maybe even politically astute, but the minute a cop was taking heat, involved in a tough shoot or accused of going overboard on an arrest, you could expect that she'd throw that cop under the bus.

In fact, many of the old-timers on the job joked that their new police commissioner was an "affirmative action hire." So they had to bust a gut when less than a year into her tenure, the Massachusetts

Association of Minority Law Enforcement Officers announced a symbolic "vote of no confidence" in O'Toole because while she promoted more minorities than her predecessors she wasn't promoting them high enough up the command ladder.

In addition to the usual police fuck-ups that O'Toole was regularly paying public penance for, there was one particularly egregious incident in which a twenty-one-year-old Emerson College student named Victoria Snelgrove was killed when police shot her with a pepper pellet during a riot after a Red Sox win. It was a freak accident. The missiles were fired from guns that release pepper spray intended to disperse crowds. The pellets weren't supposed to be like bullets, but the cop who shot Snelgrove wasn't trained properly, didn't know that the pellet could become bullet-like if you hit someone at close range. And the worst of it was that Snelgrove's "crime" was that she was celebrating the Red Sox pennant win with thousands of others who crowded into the streets in downtown Boston. The incident put a damper on the historic run that saw the Sox win the World Series for the first time since 1918. Talk about a buzzkill. And unfortunately for O'Toole, during the two-plus years she was in power, the Sox and New England Patriots won more than their fair share of titles, ensuring that the media would reference the possibility of a repeat of the Snelgrove tragedy every time either team sniffed the playoffs.

If that wasn't bad enough, crime under O'Toole's

watch began to skyrocket, with murders hitting the decade's high in 2005 and continuing to escalate into 2006, when shootings more than doubled in the city. Some convictions of so-called "innocent" men nudged the Suffolk County District Attorney into erring on the side of caution. Caution that infuriated Boston murder cops who complained that they couldn't get an arrest warrant unless the suspect was splattered with the vic's blood and was still holding the murder weapon.

In May 2006, O'Toole abruptly turned in her resignation, twenty-seven months after becoming the first female police commissioner in BPD history. There were a series of high-profile scandals that browbeat her into leaving. Her fingerprint unit had been shuttered and she spent millions in tax dollars flying in politically-connected outsiders from a private company to try to clean up that mess. There were federal contracts awarded to some of her cronies, lucrative deals that some cops saw as a quid-pro-quo nightmare. When offered the position of chief inspector of Ireland's 12,000-member national police force, the Garda Siochana, she jumped at it. Given the week she endured prior to quitting, Ireland and the thousands of miles of sea between the Emerald Isle and Boston was looking pretty inviting by then. In fact, she couldn't have picked a worse week in which the news that she was talking to Irish officials and contemplating taking a job overseas slowly began to leak out. As the *Boston Herald* put it a few days before she announced her resignation, "The Hub plummeted into its deadliest period of 2006 last week, with seven homicides on city streets, as Police Commissioner Kathleen O'Toole's standing plunged into uncertainty."

It didn't help that on the deadliest of those deadly days, when three people were murdered in the same shootout, O'Toole was accepting a crystal bowl with her name inscribed on it from a ladies' group at an event in Marblehead, a tony waterfront community twenty miles outside of Boston.

Though it was rumored that even Mayor Thomas Menino, nicknamed "Mumbles" by cruel critics because he talks like he has a mouthful of marbles, had finally lost faith in his police commissioner, at a press conference where O'Toole announced her resignation he made nice-nice with her.

"She's a good ambassador to the neighborhoods," Menino remarked. "We've had a good relationship."

Reporters in the room had to stifle a giggle as the Mayor continued. "It's a blow to me personally and professionally. She leaves behind a great command staff."

The truth was that the command staff was another issue that had driven a wedge between O'Toole and the mayor. She had created camps at BPD headquarters with two commanders, in a classic Massachusetts political fashion, starting a fracture within the highest echelons of the force. The result was a lack of solid leadership that trickled down onto the streets. No one knew who really was in charge. Morale was at an all-time low, the papers would write. The city had just begun its financial free-fall, the police head count had plummeted and the crime rate was surging. No wonder O'Toole wanted out. The question was, who would be crazy enough to replace her?

A *Boston Herald* editorial offered that, "It is a safe bet that whoever replaces Police Commissioner Kathleen O'Toole will start wondering at some point whether he or she should have taken that offer to head up a patrol in the Sunni Triangle. Running the Boston Police Department is the Bermuda Triangle of law enforcement management."

On her way out the door, O'Toole told the *London Daily Mail* that "the last twenty-seven months have been a difficult time." Given the state Boston and the BPD were in, O'Toole admitted that, "I don't envy the mayor and I don't envy my successor."

That was the environment that Ed Davis willingly walked into in December 2006 when he took over the country's twentieth largest (and they claim the oldest) police force, one that was nearly ten times the size of the 240-officer department he just left.

On his way in the door, the rangy Davis tried to strike the perfect balance with his first comments as PC.

"I am honored that Mayor Menino has entrusted me to the lead the historic Boston Police Department."

"The department has been recognized internationally as a model for neighborhood policing. This model was built on community partnerships. I will reaffirm that commitment, especially to the neighborhoods most impacted by crime."

"Increasing community trust in police has always been my top priority."

"I come from a family of police, so I understand the needs of the police officer on the street."

Ed Davis had his work cut out for him. He said he was ready for it. But people wondered if an outsider was up to the task. After all, heading the BPD was so difficult, some say impossible, that its last two commissioners not only fled Boston but the country once they'd had enough of the job. Paul Evans, the commissioner before O'Toole, ended his tenure by running off to a job in London. It seemed that former Boston police commissioners couldn't get far enough away from the Hub.

However, Davis vowed not to be chased off. He started his career as a cop in Lowell in 1978 and soon earned the same reputation bestowed upon his father, a "squared-away cop," the highest compliment cops give to other cops. He worked patrol, as a detective, undercover, as a sergeant and up the command ranks, 28 years in all. The last twelve of those he headed the Lowell Police, during which time the exact opposite of what was going on in Boston in 2006 happened in Lowell: Crime went down by 60 percent. Davis said that decline was the result of "community policing," getting cops out of their patrol cars and walking beats where they can meet the people in the neighborhood, gain their trust and eventually form alliances that provide the information a cop needs not only to make arrests but head off some crime before it happens.

The crime reductions didn't go without notice. Davis had been a finalist in 2004 for the Boston police commissioner job but Menino picked O'Toole instead.

And when he finally got the top job in Boston, Davis achieved something that none of his recent predecessors could. In his first few years he received relatively high marks from the media and law enforcement observers, no small feat that. The Boston Police Department has what some say is an overly powerful union, the Boston Police Patrolmen's Association. And like most things Boston, the BPD officers often get tagged with what is ultimately an unfair reputation, being more racist than other big-city police departments. That reputation causes tensions, to say the least, in Boston's poorest and highest-crime neighborhoods, which are almost exclusively communities of color. Because of this, any Boston police commissioner who expects to succeed must learn how to walk a fine line between placating the police union and the leaders of the city's poorest neighborhoods. Much of the time, it's a no-win situation, as O'Toole found out. When a controversy arises, if you back your cops, the poor communities are up in arms, and vice versa. But through his first two and a half years on the job, Davis proved to be a fairly adept tightrope walker. He even developed a decent relationship with the head of the police union, Tom Nee—a well-respected lifelong cop who also had been elected President of the National Association of Police Officers. Tom Nee had pull across the country and the last thing you wanted to do was annoy him. O'Toole bent over backward to make Nee happy. Davis was not going to bend over like that but he tried to make some concessions that recognized how hardworking his rank-and-file cops were. He was one, after all.

For example, after one scandal Davis came up with a policy calling for any of his officers to be fired for "testilying," lying while testifying at trial, or putting false information in a police report to bolster their cases. Nee was furious. But then that anger felt by cops was assuaged, albeit slightly, when Davis stuck up for his guys when Conley wanted the State Police to usurp their right to investigate homicides in Boston parks and on city buses. Davis also recognized the suicide of a young female police officer who had been the first to arrive at the scene of a bomb squad cop's murder in 1991 as a line-of-duty death because she had been so traumatized by that response. The people who loved Denise Corbett, the officer who took her own life weeks before Davis was even sworn in, appreciated the fact that Davis made sure her family was taken care of. She had a husband, also a Boston cop, and kids—two of whom were severely autistic. That was a stand-up move and one that was appreciated by the cops on the beat.

And whether it was because of his community policing philosophy or just because crime can be unexplainably cyclical, the number of murders, rapes, shootings and other crimes actually began to decrease under Davis.

But like being a professional athlete, being a police commissioner is a what-have-you-done-for-me-lately job. On April 14, 2009, a single crime threatened to wipe out all of the modest successes that Davis achieved since becoming head honcho. And though they had vastly improved their arrest and conviction rates over the past couple years, the homicide detectives knew that all their hard work would be for naught and that *that* dreaded tag could resurface as fast as it took a headline writer to type in "Worst homicide squad in America" again. If the BPD did not identify and arrest the Craigslist Killer soon, then Davis might as well have started an overseas job search as well.

That's why after he got the call from Sgt. Brian Albert, the man that Davis had appointed to lead the newly-formed Boston Police fugitive squad, that the Craigslist Killer was in their sights, the commissioner looked at his deputy superintendent and right-hand man Dan Linskey and said, "Let's take a ride."

By the time the police commissioner and his deputy arrived, there were two dozen cops now scattered

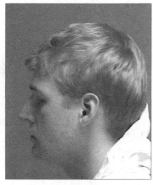

Philip Markoff on the day of his arrest, in a tyvec suit, after his clothes were confiscated by the Boston Police Department.　　　*Courtesy of the Boston Police Department*

Announcement of the arrest of Philip Markoff in April 2009.
Courtesy of The Boston Herald / *photo by Mark Garfinkle*

Police believe Markoff played blackjack at Foxwoods in Connecticut and stayed at the MGM Grand shortly after each of the incidents they were investigating.

Photo taken by Michele McPhee

Suffolk County District Attorney Dan Conley announcing the arrest of Markoff on charges of armed robbery, kidnapping, and the murder of Julissa Brisman. The public learned the suspect was a Boston University medical student.
Courtesy of
The Boston Herald/*Photo by Mark Garfinkle*

Boston Police Commissioner Ed Davis talking about the around-the-clock investigation into the Craigslist Killer after Markoff was arrested on his way to Foxwoods Casino in Connecticut.

Courtesy of The Boston Herald / *photo by Nancy Lane*

A Most Wanted Poster released by Boston Police after another exotic dancer was bound in an attempted robbery at the Holiday Inn Express in Warwick, Rhode Island.

Courtesy of the Boston Police Department

Police in front of the Warwick, Rhode Island Holiday Inn Express after an exotic dancer called them to say she had a ball-gag stuffed into her mouth by an assailant who answered her Craigslist ad. The April 16, 2009 attack was thwarted by her husband. *Courtesy of* The Boston Herald

Markoff listens next to his attorney John Salsberg as charges are read against him.
Courtesy of
The Boston Herald / *photo by Mark Garfinkle*

Hector Brisman shields his face as his daughter's accused killer is escorted into court.

Courtesy of The Boston Herald / *photo by Mark Garfinkle*

Markoff announces that he is not guilty of the charges leveled against him.

Courtesy of The Boston Herald / *photo by Mark Garfinkle*

John Salsberg escorts Markoff's brother and sister-in-law into the Nashua Street jail in Boston. Markoff told them: "Forget about me. More is coming out."

Courtesy of The Boston Herald / *photo by John Wilcox*

Megan McAllister leaving the Nashua Street jail after she broke up with Markoff. She emerged with her mother—and without her engagement ring. *Courtesy of WBZ-TV / Boston*

The Nashua Street jail, where Philip Markoff will be held from the time of his April 2009 arrest until his pending trial. *Photo taken by Michele McPhee*

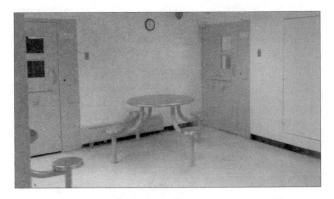

The cell at the Nashua Street jail where Markoff will be held until his trial. *From the library of Michele McPhee*

around 8 Highpoint Circle. There was an assistant district attorney from Dan Conley's office there. Everyone was in place. But they were going to take their time. This was a high publicity case with reporters from across the country ready to dissect any investigative missteps. They had to be positive that the blond guy with the pretty girlfriend was, in fact, the same man photographed at the Westin Hotel on April 10; the same guy photographed text-messaging someone on April 14 at the Marriott Copley; the same guy who was identified by a stripper in Rhode Island as the man who robbed her at gunpoint and tried to stuff a ball gag into her mouth on April 16.

Davis and Albert wanted to move in and arrest the man they had identified as Philip Markoff immediately. But before Dan Conley would give the go-ahead he had to pull one more power play, show Davis who really was in charge.

"Get me a positive identification," Conley told Davis.

It was another frustrating delay for the cops who were positive by then they had the right guy. Cell phone records showed his phone pinging off towers not far from the crime scenes, and the IP address used to contact murder victim Julissa Brisman had been traced to his building. He fit the description of a six-foot-three blond man with light-colored skin and a lanky build that his victims had described. He also looked "stressed," one cop on the scene would later say.

The woman with him, however, was oblivious to her boyfriend's stiffness. She was "giggling and flirting and hanging all over him," a cop in on the tail said. "He was essentially ignoring her but she didn't care. She was all lovey-dovey and his body language said, 'Get off me.' It was a weird dynamic to watch. She was in love, she was in a fairy tale and he looked like he was going to snap."

The target had emerged from the building. His smitten girlfriend at his side. They were carrying a suitcase.

It was Monday, April 20, six days after Julissa Brisman was beaten and shot to death in a luxury Boston hotel, and more than two days since the stakeout in front of Markoff's building began. By then the cops were chomping at the bit to take the Craigslist Killer offline but Conley wouldn't give the go-ahead.

The cops watched as Philip Markoff climbed behind the wheel of a Toyota Corolla that was registered to a woman named Megan McAllister. Had to be the giggly girl, the cops who ran the plates figured.

At that point, the cops had no idea whether McAllister knew what Markoff had been up to. Was she the Bonnie to his Clyde? Could she be helping him try to escape at this very minute? It was hard to imagine that she knew nothing about the so-called Craigslist Killer. Had she picked up the *Boston Herald* or the *Boston Globe* at any time over the past week she would have seen a grainy, but unmistakable, image of her fiancé on the front page. Rhode Island investigators had released images of the suspect who had attacked a woman at the Warwick, Rhode Island, Holiday Inn and those pictures fueled the media frenzy. Every television newscast, local and national, lead with the story. There were pictures of the Craigslist Killer everywhere.

Conley was continuing to push Davis's buttons. He would not give the okay to pull over the suspect and arrest him until they had another confirmation from Trisha Leffler, the prostitute from Las Vegas who had been held captive by her assailant for fifteen minutes and robbed on April 10 in another Boston luxury hotel. He wanted Leffler to look at another photo array that included pictures of Philip Markoff provided to police by Boston University. Boston Police officials were furious, but Conley would not approve the takedown until there was another photo array conducted. He wanted detectives to stack eight photos one on top of another—a technique that he had adopted during the rift with Davis months earlier, and one that homicide investigators were somewhat suspicious of. It had been developed by a psychology professor named Dr. Gary Wells who came up with the technique at Iowa State on the theory that the ensuing identification is purer. But most cops hate change and figured if some college egghead came up with it, then this procedure had to make it harder to pick out the perp.

But the cops in this case had no choice. No photo showing equaled no Markoff arrest. One cop on the stakeout remembered half hoping that Markoff and his fiancé could jump on a plane and disappear so that Conley would get blamed for screwing up their case. Again.

Leffler flipped the cards, all blond frat-boy-looking men, and when she got to Markoff's college identification she stopped. "That's absolutely him."

That information was transmitted to Lieutenant Bobby Merner, who immediately radioed Albert.

The time was 4:10 p.m. Adrenaline coursed through the veins of the police officers who had been simply sitting and watching for days. Finally, it was time to move in. Go time.

Markoff was behind the wheel of the gray Toyota Corolla registered to a Megan McAllister of Little Silver, New Jersey, when he heard the cacophony of sirens behind him. He pulled to the side of the road on I-95 South in Walpole, Massachusetts. Ironically, the town was home to MCI-Cedar Junction, the highest security prison in Massachusetts. It was known as Walpole, and the very name of the town was synonymous with scumbags: killers, pedophiles . . . the worst of the worst. The cops did not intentionally pull the suspect over in Walpole. They simply wanted to nab him before he crossed the border into Rhode Island, which would have created a jurisdictional nightmare for the Boston police. But it was sweet to contemplate that they would be able to put this smirking frat boy away in the prison right where they stopped him for the rest of his life.

As the police approached him, guns drawn, Markoff did not say a word. Megan did plenty of talking for both of them. She wailed and pleaded and begged cops to tell her what was going on.

Merner kept it simple as his beefy hands secured the cuffs around Markoff's wrists. "Philip Markoff. You are under arrest for the murder of Julissa Brisman on April 14, 2009," Merner said.

"Murder," Megan McAllister screamed through sobs. "You have the wrong guy. You have the wrong guy."

Investigators ignored her. They were fairly certain they had the right guy. The arrest was not based just on Leffler's photo identification. They had cell phone records, witness statements, his Internet fingerprints as well as the good old-fashioned kind. A very clear fingerprint lifted from the duct tape that the assailant had used to cover Leffler's mouth. Rhode Island police had also lifted a fingerprint from the stairwell of the Warwick, Rhode Island, hotel that had matched the earlier crime. One of the zip-ties used in Rhode Island also had a print.

Cops bundled both Markoff and McAllister into one of the unmarked cars. Her car was towed back to Boston police headquarters until investigators could get a search warrant. Then they went over the car with a fine-toothed comb. A criminal complaint with Markoff's name on it had already been written up:

Philip Markoff
8 Highpoint Circle
Quincy, MA 02169
Date of Birth: 2/12/1986
Gender: Male
Race: White
Height: 6'3"
Weight: 205 pounds
Eyes: Blue
Hair: Blonde or Strawberry
Police Department: Boston PD Area D-4
Officer ID: 8220
CC Num: 090190621
Complainant: Daniel M. Keeler

Once they arrived back at Boston Police Headquarters Megan continued to weep. Markoff said nothing. He appeared despondent, even catatonic, cops would later remember.

Soon the Boston Police Department released a press statement:

DEATH INVESTIGATION AT THE CO- PLEY MARRIOTT HOTEL SUSPECT CHARGED WITH JULISSA BRISMAN'S MURDER

Boston Police Commissioner Edward Davis and Suffolk County District Attorney Daniel

Conley today announced the arrest of **Philip Markoff, 23, of Quincy** with the murder of Julissa Brisman at the Copley Marriott Hotel on April 14, 2009 and the armed robbery and kidnapping of an additional victim on April 10, 2009 at the Westin Hotel.

Markoff was taken into custody at approximately 4:00pm this afternoon and formerly charged this evening. The charges are based on forensic and electronic evidence developed during the around the clock investigation that continues tonight and will continue in the weeks and months to come. Markoff is expected to face arraignment in the Boston Municipal Court tomorrow morning.

Commissioner Davis and District Attorney Conley wish to thank the following agencies for their invaluable assistance during the course of this complex investigation: Warwick Police Department, Massachusetts Attorney General's Office, Massachusetts State Police, Federal Bureau of Investigation, United States Secret Service, MBTA Transit Police, Boston University Police Department, US Marshals, Quincy Police Department and the New York Police Department.

The Boston Police Homicide Unit is actively investigating the facts and circumstances of this incident and urges anyone with information regarding this incident to notify them by calling (617) 343-4470. Individuals wishing to provide information anonymously may do so by calling the CrimeStoppers Tip Line at 1-800-494-TIPS or texting 'TIP' to CRIME (27463). The Boston Police strictly protects the identity of all individuals wishing to provide information anonymously.

Those tips would start to fly in as Megan told the officers that she had spent the week prior—the week of her fiancé's alleged crime spree—planning her wedding at her parent's house. *They could check that. Call her mother.* The suitcases? What about them? They were going to Foxwoods for a romantic weekend. What of it? They had a reservation at the MGM Grand. Check it out.

At that point, she was 100 percent confident that everything was a big mistake. Had to be. She even blurted out to investigators that her mother had warned her when she was coming back to Quincy. "Be careful. Someone was killed up there in Boston," her mother said.

She had no idea, of course, that her fiancé was the prime suspect in the crime that her mother had been worried about. That he would be dragged into a Boston courtroom the very next day where he would be arraigned on murder charges.

The police didn't have any evidence linking her

to Markoff's crimes. They told her they were going to let her go but not her fiancé. At that point, she became hysterical.

"I want to go home," she wept. Cops let her borrow a computer so she could book a flight back to New Jersey. A patrol officer drove her to Logan Airport. She was still wearing her engagement ring when she boarded the plane. She would continue to wear it. For a while at least.

As she left Boston, Philip Markoff was being booked. As his fingertips were rolled against a pad so they could be matched against the latent prints lifted at the crime scenes cops told him they needed to take pictures of his skin. He was asked to strip down to his underwear and was given a white paper jumpsuit to pull on.

Cops wanted to photograph his skin for a reason. Julissa Brisman had the skin of her assailant lodged under her long nails. She had scratched the man who murdered her.

And the cops couldn't help but notice that Philip Markoff had welts on his neck. They wanted to take a look at his chest too.

In his mug shot taken at Boston Police headquarters that afternoon, the paper suit was clearly visible in the shots taken of Markoff's face from the front and his profile. What was not immediately visible were the scratches. But they were there, and the photos taken of the raised skin that Markoff had studied in the mirror at Foxwoods would become part of the growing mountain of evidence against him as the Craigslist Killer.

Markoff then asked the police where he would be going that night.

"Nashua Street jail," Bobby Merner responded.

The suspect, still wearing what police called a Tyvec suit because his clothes had been seized as evidence, made another request to the police: "Can I go to the bathroom first." He was escorted to a men's room in the booking location at One Schroeder Plaza. Cops had read him his rights and Markoff was allowed to make a phone call home—prompting his mother to reach out to a man she had very little contact with, his father, her ex-husband. His brother was also called. They would be flying to Boston that very day after they were told Markoff would be in a Boston courtroom to be arraigned on murder and armed robbery charges.

A patrolman was given the task of standing outside the bathroom door to make sure nothing happened to Markoff as he used the toilet. That's when he heard the roll of toilet paper spinning followed by tearing sounds. Markoff was balling up TP and stuffing it down his pants.

"I might need this later," he told the cops.

Ostensibly, there seemed to be nothing dangerous about toilet paper. So the cop let it pass and let him keep the wads of toilet paper. Deputy sheriffs assigned to the Suffolk County Sherriff's Office headed by

Andrea Cabral were not as lenient. As overseers of the Suffolk County Jail, a place that houses about 1,000 pretrial detainees in thirteen different units, they had seen it all. They knew what could be fashioned into a weapon and what could be used by a distraught first-timer to try to kill himself. Toilet papers could easily be wadded up and swallowed. They made him throw the toilet paper out before he was escorted into a general population area.

He wouldn't last there long, though. His toilet paper plan may have been foiled but other suicide attempts were to come.

11

Back in New Jersey, Megan McAllister could not
sleep at all. Not even for a second. Murder, kidnapping, guns, hookers, robbery, a ball gag! For chris-
sakes, where did it end? The man she was going to
marry, the man who helped her select china for their
upcoming wedding, who brought her flowers and
breakfast in bed? The man who had rented a horse
and buggy to propose to her, who said she could
have a wedding party with nineteen people including
three flower girls and two ring bearers, who told her
every day how beautiful she was? The tall, handsome and caring doctor-in-training? The guy who
texted her sweet messages, things like, "I luv you
too. :x" that police now say he was typing nonchalantly minutes after killing a young masseuse named
Julissa Brisman?

Who was this man?

Their history flashed through her mind all night
long. Nothing. There was no indication that the Philip

Markoff she had grown to love and planned to marry in a few short months and spend the rest of her life with was capable of any of the things this Craigslist Killer character had done.

This was not her Philip Markoff. Had to be a mistake. She wished she could talk to him. Wished he could defend his good name, the name of a future doctor. Someone had to do something. With Philip behind bars and unable to fight back against these this scurrilous allegations, the future Mrs. Philip Markoff took on the role of protector. She typed up a quick email and sent it to a "contact us" prompt at ABC News's *Good Morning America*:

"Unfortunately you were given wrong information as was the public," McAllister wrote in the email. "All I have to say to you is Philip is a beautiful person inside and out and could not hurt a fly! A police officer in Boston (or many) is trying to make big bucks by selling this false story to the TV stations. What else is new?? Philip is an intelligent man who is just trying to live his life so if you could leave us alone we would greatly appreciate it. We expect to marry in August and share a wonderful, meaningful life together."

The *Boston Herald*'s headline on the morning of April 21, 2009, read: "Craigslist Killer Caught! BU med student nabbed in hub hotel slay."

McAllister ripped off another email to the newspaper. "I will stand by Philip as I know he's innocent. He is a beautiful man inside and out. He's intelligent and loyal and the best fiancé that a woman could ask for. Philip would not hurt a fly."

She next contacted *People* magazine. "Philip is a beautiful man inside and out and did not commit this crime. Unfortunately, someone else did and needs to be penalized."

Throngs of reporters were staked out in front of her parents' home. Megan grew up in a tight-knit family well insulated from any of the things that the Craigslist Killer had been accused of. So she became myopic and steadfastly refused to believe anything the police were saying about her beloved Philip was true.

Her intentions were good, but the emails defending her "beautiful man inside and out" to the media were like throwing chum to a school of sharks. Great whites at that.

In fact, the media circus became so large and loud that that morning—hours before the man who had very nearly become his son-in-law would be charged with murder, armed robbery and kidnapping in a Boston courtroom—Jim McAllister was forced to address the phalanx of reporters camped out on his street. He had a simple statement as he spoke to the scrum of reporters as photographers clicked away. He spoke with assuredness. Jim McAllister was not a man to be trifled with. It was a difficult task to not offend his daughter, even if he would have been justified if he wanted to strangle Philip Markoff with his bare hands for what he did, both to those poor young women he was accused of attacking and his daughter.

"We will have no comment about how Megan is doing," McAllister said, visibly rattled by the scene that played out in front of his neighbors. But he was not going to back down to these cretin camped out at the end of his driveway. "Other than to say, as expected, not well." Jim McAllister obviously wanted to be completely supportive of his daughter at a time when her world seemed to be crumbling down all around her. However, he didn't appear to have his daughter's unwavering belief that the police had arrested the wrong man.

"She's still confident in Phil, other than that we are saying a lot of prayers," he said. "She's got a lot of friends, lot of family . . . that's been a big help to us. That's been wonderful."

Then came the question that was on everyone's mind: *Did she know what her fiancé, the man she lived with, had been up to?*

"Absolutely not," McAllister barked. Then he stormed away from the microphones that had been set up at the end of the driveway and went back into the house to comfort his devastated daughter.

The Boston police investigators who had handled McAllister with kid gloves were surprised at the tenor of her anger toward the police and her accusation that they were trying to make money selling their story (which cops were prohibited from doing anyway). They could have held her too, made her life miserable, forced her to call a lawyer and post bail. Instead they let her use their computer to book a flight home, then drove her to the airport. Of course, they could understand her confusion. By then investigators truly believed she didn't know anything about the crimes and could sympathize with the devastation she must be going through while she struggled to come to terms with the fact that her fiancé was living a double life. Sure, when they observed her she looked like "she was living in a fairy tale," as one cop would come to remark. A fairy tale that had turned into a horror story.

And it was about to get scarier.

Megan McAllister should be grateful she went home. Because what police would find when they executed a search warrant at their small apartment would turn her stomach. The apartment was sparsely furnished. It didn't have any of the fancy trappings that McAllister was hoping to get as wedding gifts in August. One of the couple's neighbors, Jonathan Uva, said that he heard crime scene investigators rifling through their apartment from Sunday night into early Monday morning. He was not exactly friends with Markoff, but they had become "hallway acquaintances" just by living in the same building. Hi, how ya doing, nice day, bye. That kind of stuff. The fact that Markoff was arrested as the Craigslist Killer came as a complete shocker. Why didn't he see the similarities between Markoff and the suspect, whose photos had been on the front pages of newspapers across the country since April 14th, the day 25-year-old Julissa Brisman had been discovered dead? Uva didn't really read the story all that closely and never studied the pictures. And why should he have any reason to believe his polite, mild-mannered neighbor was a killer? The whole thing, he said, just seemed surreal. The images of the Craigslist Killer were quite literally the guy next door; the handsome med student with the hot fiancé who had been to his house for parties in the past.

"I can't even put it into words, the disbelief I'm putting into words right now," Uva told *Good Morning America* (GMA). "It's just a total disconnect from what we're hearing in the news."

"I'm a little unsettled, definitely," he said. Another friend, Mike Dye, told GMA that he'd had Markoff over to his apartment for parties and for the Super Bowl. "I like to think I'm a good judge of character, hang out with people who are similar to myself," he said. "Didn't suspect anything like that."

"I would never believe this would be something he would do," friend Kym Direnzo told reporters. Markoff's Facebook profile had listed hundreds of friends who attend schools in Boston and upstate New York. But for all the nice things they had to say about Markoff, there was an aloofness to him. He seemed to them to be something of a mystery, though nothing overtly nefarious. Some of his friends went as far to say they didn't even know he and McAllister were engaged. Though they agreed Philip and Megan seemed like a nice, normal couple, his friends said they thought the two were simply dating.

"He very rarely talked about himself," Uva said.

What could he possibly say? Would he reveal details about his sexual desires or that he spent way too much time at Foxwoods, even though he had $130,000 in outstanding student loans? No. It was much easier for his neighbors and classmates to see him only as a second-year medical student with a promising future, engaged to a beautiful woman. Boston University was just as stunned.

Markoff was a medical student in excellent standing. He was slated to begin an internship in the very emergency room where his victim was pronounced dead. He was engaged. His wedding was going to be held in an upscale hotel on the Jersey Shore. The wedding band couldn't be more all-American: a cover band of freaking Bruce Springsteen. His girlfriend was classy. His college record impeccable. This suspect never even had his car booted and towed, a rite of passage for Boston college students who racked up parking tickets in the area and never paid them.

Christ. Even Barack Obama—the President of the United States—got jammed up with the Somerville parking clerk's office. He had been written up an astonishing 17 times for illegally parking while a student at Harvard University and never paid the tickets. That is, not until two weeks before he announced he was going to seek the Democratic nod to become a Presidential contender. Two weeks before his official announcement, Obama coughed up $400 in parking ticket fines. He got off easy. Somehow late fees that would have buried the average guy vanished when Obama's staffer showed up to pay the tickets he got near his Somerville home at 365 Broadway where he lived while attending Harvard University Law School. Between October 5, 1988, and January 12, 1990, Obama got whacked with seventeen traffic violations, sometimes committing two infractions in the same day. The abuses included parking in a resident permit area, parking in a bus stop and failing to pay the meter. Twelve of Obama's seventeen tickets were given to him on Massachusetts Avenue—not far from the university. In one eight-day stretch in 1988, Obama was cited seven times for parking violations and was fined $45. Thirteen of the seventeen violations occurred within one month in 1988. The tickets went unpaid for over seventeen years and $260 in late fees were added to the tab. On Jan. 26, 2008, the fines and late fees were paid in full. At the time, Obama spokeswoman Jennifer Psaki said the presidential candidate's parking violations were not relevant. "He didn't owe that much and what he did owe, he paid," Psaki said. "Many people have parking tickets and late fees."

Obama has more trouble with the law in Massachusetts than Markoff had. Until now.

Markoff was like the invisible man. He floated through Boston University Medical School without accruing a disciplinary record and was so advanced

academically at SUNY Albany that he graduated a
year early. Boston University Medical School was so
embarrassed that the employees at the admissions
office were accused by journalists at the *Daily Free
Press*, the college paper, of throwing out copies of the
paper with references to the murder. Medical campus
provost and the medical school's dean Karen Antman
released one statement, dated April 20. It reads, in
its entirety: "Phillip [sic] H. Markoff is a second
year medical student at Boston University School of
Medicine. Upon learning of the charges against him,
University officials immediately suspended him. Any
further inquiries on this case should be directed to
the Boston Police Department."

It was difficult to locate a copy of the college
paper anywhere where there could be prospective
new students—meaning an influx of new money.
Parents writing huge checks to Boston University were
certainly not going to be assuaged with headlines like
"Police Arrest BU Student as Craigslist Killer."

School officials could be shocked and surprised,
but there was at least one woman who saw through
the façade long before Philip Markoff would come
to be known as the Craigslist Killer.

Morgan Houston had attended SUNY Albany
with Markoff and graduated with him in 2007. She
saw the surveillance photos as she spent April vaca-
tion with her parents at their Aiken, South Carolina,
summer home. "I ran downstairs. I woke up my mom
and said, 'Mom, can you believe this?' " Houston told

the *New York Daily News*. "We turned on the TV and the pictures from security—they look like him. Knowing him, especially if you see his profile, it looks like him. It was Phil."

Houston's mother knew exactly who "Phil" was. She remembers the night she got a tearful phone call from her daughter at college. Her friend had pinned her up against a wall one dark night after they had attended a party together. He was one of those guys who did not have a filter, who behaved inappropriately around women. He showed up at one Halloween party dressed as a mammogram and tried to give women free breast exams. It was raunchy, frat-boy behavior, sure, but Markoff took it a step, or two, too far and it took on a more sinister tone.

"Some people are adamant there's no way he could have done this—it's Phil; he couldn't hurt a fly," Houston said.

Houston, however, was one of those people who thought that Markoff had shown signs of a dark side.

"And then there's other people that have seen bits and glimpses and the memories are coming back," she told the *News*. "I had really passed that situation out of my mind."

Megan McAllister would eventually have to do the same thing. Put her relationship with Philip Markoff out of her mind. Especially after news broke about what police found in the apartment they shared, under their bed. She had no idea, in fact, how he came to be carrying $4,500 in cash at the time of his arrest when they were pulled over on Interstate 95 South. And she certainly didn't know that Philip had taken a scalpel to his copy of *Gray's Anatomy* and chunked out the pages to fit the 9mm handgun police were saying was the weapon used to murder Julissa Brisman. The weapon discovered in the hollowed-out medical school book was quite literally the smoking gun that investigators were hoping for. In fact, they were astonished that someone who was so smart, a guy who had been accepted to a prestigious medical school, could be stupid enough to leave evidence of his alleged crimes all over his apartment.

"It was like a part of him wanted to get caught," a cop would tell a reporter in a barroom in an exchange known as a "dead-man conversation," meaning that it was on background and the investigator could never be revealed as a source. "It also showed that the fiancée was living in la-la land. He must have known that he had her utmost trust if he was hiding guns and other women's panties in their home."

Police also found plastic zip-ties exactly like the ones used to bound the three victims linked to the Craigslist Killer and duct tape, the same brand that the handsome john had slapped over Trisha Leffler, the Las Vegas prostitute who was bound and robbed in the Westin Copley hotel four days before Julissa's murder. Most disturbing, though, at least to Megan McAllister, were the sixteen pairs of panties that were found in rolled-up pairs of socks. Two of the panties looked suspiciously like the ones that were stolen from Leffler's room. Others, though, were not at all identifiable. Julissa Brisman's killer did not have time to rifle through her belongings to steal panties. The deadly struggle took place in the foyer of her room. Cynthia Melton, the Rhode Island stripper and lap dance specialist who the Craigslist Killer tried to rob two days after the murder, said her attacker didn't steal any of her underwear. He got scared off by her husband moments after he entered her room. So whose panties, fourteen pair, were they?

To investigators Markoff's panty stash could only suggest one thing: There were other victims.

"This is a brutal, vicious, savage attack. This suspect showed he was willing to take advantage of women," District Attorney Dan Conley said. Then he added, chillingly, that there was "a strong possibility he has done this before."

"We urge anyone who has encountered this suspect to come forward," Conley said. The district attorney went so far as say that anyone in the sex trade industry who was also victimized by the Criagslist Killer would be granted "full immunity" from prosecution in connection with their prostitution acts if they cooperated.

"He is a very dangerous man," Conley said. "We have the evidence to prove it."

12

The fifth-floor courtroom at Suffolk Superior Court was absolutely packed on April 21, 2009. The standing-room-only crowd was not there to see the usual riffraff and good-for-nothings that typically shuffled in and out of Justice Paul K. Leary's courtroom: small-time drug dealers, burglars, stick-up boys, persistent offenders of all stripes.

On this day the crowd, which included a heavy contingency of media members from all around the northeast, was there to see one man plead guilty or innocent to the accusation that he was the infamous Craigslist Killer.

Alongside the throng of media, who moved their heads in unison like spectators at a tennis match every time a new prisoner was escorted by court officers into the courtroom from a side door, were Philip Markoff's parents. His father, Richard Markoff, was literally sweating it out; beads of perspiration gathered on top of his bald dome and trickled down into the unkempt tufts of hair that horseshoed around the sides and back of his head.

Richard Markoff continually removed his glasses and nervously wiped them and fidgeted with his mustache uncomfortably as reporters stared at him. Occasionally, one would sidle up to him trying to get a quote about his son, requests that were refused with a small shake of his head. Next to him sat his ex-wife, Susan Haynes, who wore the nondescript uniform of a suburban middle-aged mom with a tan sweater and simple black skirt. She was clearly not a woman who spent a lot of time on her appearance or dress. She carried a fake leather bag that matched her sensible shoes. Her dirty blonde hair was shoulder-length, parted on the left and combed across her forehead in a dowdy fashion. Like her ex-husband, she wore wire-rimmed glasses.

It was hard to imagine that a good-looking man like Philip was sired by this absolutely plain-looking couple. Where Philip was tall and lean, his father was short and a bit paunchy. If Philip's looks favored either of them it was his mother, who one might call handsome.

His brother Jonathan was also in the courtroom, sitting at his father's left side in a crisp suit. Jon's appearance was an extraordinary gesture of brotherly love given the fact that he and Philip had stopped speaking to each other for reasons only the two of them knew some time ago. In fact, the brothers hadn't been close since they were kids, with Jon deciding to live with their father after the Markoffs divorced and Philip opting to stay with their mom.

Jon was polished with a slick trendy haircut, a bit spiky on top with hipster sideburns. He sported an expensive watch on a hand that clung to that of his wife, Deanna, a pretty blonde woman who looked stunned to find herself in a criminal courtroom awaiting the arraignment of her brother-in-law on murder charges. She stared everywhere but at the box where Phil would stand in short time, accused of murder.

Markoff's parents sat side-by-side and held hands but did not speak, even when Magistrate Judge Gary D. Wilson came into the room and his clerk started calling cases for Leary's courtroom. They also did not react when there as an audible gasp in the room as Julissa Brisman's father Hector Guzman arrived with his daughter, Julissa's little sister, Melissa, escorted into the courtroom by homicide investigators Bob Kenney and Lieutenant Detective Bob Merner.

For all of the people who crammed into the small courtroom there was one conspicuous absence. Megan McAllister—Markoff's fiancée who had spent the previous night and that morning emailing the media, asserting that her man was innocent and sweet and "wouldn't hurt a fly"—did not show up to court. In fact, outside his family, there was not one single friend there to support Markoff.

The courtroom was so crowded some reporters were relegated to the back. The judge was agitated at the noise and he tried his best to move Markoff's case up the docket to get the scrum of reporters out of there in an effort to restore his courtroom to its mundane routine of processing the city's petty, run-of-the-mill criminals. When the judge's clerk called out docket number 09-104-79 followed by Markoff's name, the room went silent with anticipation. The six-foot-three man—wearing tan khakis and a blue and white striped button-down shirt along with hand-cuffs and leg shackles—was escorted by the elbow into the room. In those preppy clothes and with his hair tousled as always, he looked more like a yuppie frat boy who had been busted for "lewd and lascivious" after getting drunk and urinating in the bushes near Fenway Park than a cold-blooded murderer. He towered over the beefy court officers flanking him. He did not even glance at his parents, which was odd. Most murder suspects tried to allay their fear, their anxiety, maybe even their anger by searching out their loved ones for moral support. But Philip didn't look their way once. Not even a cursory glance.

He had been assigned one of the city's most formidable defense attorneys, John Salsberg. Salsberg, a part-time clinical instructor at Harvard Law School, had been dubbed a "Massachusetts Super Lawyer" by *Boston* magazine four years running by then and was recognized in 2005 by the Massachusetts Association of Criminal Defense Lawyers for "his tireless and courageous advocacy." He was the type of lawyer who cops hated and feared—no Boston cop wanted to be on the business end of a Salsberg cross.

He had made a name for himself representing a teenager named Kyle Bryant who had been charged as a co-conspirator in one of Boston's most notorious murder cases—the slaying of a fourteen-year-old pregnant girl who was beaten, stabbed and bludgeoned to death before being buried in a shallow grave in 1999.

Chauntae Jones was eight months pregnant when Bryant, the eighteen-year-old father of her unborn baby, and his friend Lord Hampton allegedly lured her to the edge of a hole they had dug on the grounds of a state hospital and killed her with a knife and a brick. The killing happened several weeks after a Boston juvenile court judge said at a child welfare hearing for Jones that he wanted prosecutors to investigate a statutory rape charge against Bryant.

The murder, rightfully, horrified the city.

Bryant gave detectives a tape-recorded admission that he was present when Jones was killed, though he added that it was Hampton who murdered Jones as she begged for her life. Bryant said he had nothing to do with any of it, a claim authorities thought was transparently self-serving. A pillowcase placed over the eighth grader's head matched another one found at Bryant's house and police determined the shovel found at the crime scene had come from his house.

But seemingly against all odds, Salsberg won an acquittal.

"Blind Justice: Bryant Acquitted," the *Boston Herald* screamed the next day. "Acquittal Stuns Courthouse," the *Boston Globe*'s headline cried out. The *Globe* described the verdict and fallout:

"Bryant's eyes widened when the jury foreman twice uttered the words 'not guilty,' but the 22-year-old defendant registered little emotion.

"But the verdict stunned many in the packed Suffolk Superior courtroom, including Jones' mother, Pamela Jones, who began sobbing. After the courtroom had nearly emptied, she started screaming in the hallway and had to be restrained by five court officers as she struggled to re-enter the room.

" 'Anybody can kill somebody and get away with that,' Jones' cousin, C.C. Jones screamed as tears streamed down her face."

It was of little solace to Chauntae's family that another jury later convicted Hampton of the murder. Bryant, the one they believed spearheaded Chauntae's murder to avoid a statutory rape charge, got away with murder, in the family's opinion. He was the one who got Chauntae pregnant. According to police videotape, he heard her screams for help; he did nothing to save her; he helped dig the hole. Everything people feared about Kyle Bryant would be re-examined in February 2010, when he was arrested for shooting a man dead. At the time of this writing, he remained in jail.

That case cemented Salsberg's reputation as a miracle worker for criminals. And that's what it will

take, most court observers feel, for the accused Craigslist Killer to avoid spending the rest of his days in
prison.

That day in Judge Leary's courtroom, the charges
that the clerk read off against Markoff seemed like
they'd never end.

For the murder and robbery of Julissa Brisman
at the Marriott Copley Place hotel on April 14,
2009:

Murder c265 S1": Murder Chapter c265 Section 1.
Kidnapping, Firearm-Armed": Chapter 265
    Section 26.
Assault to Rob, Armed": Chapter 265 Section 18(b).
Firearm without FID Card, Possess": Chapter
    269 Section 10 (h).

And the robbery of Trisha Leffler at the Westin
Copley Place hotel on April 10, 2009:

Robbery, Armed": Chapter 269 Section 17.
Kidnapping, Firearm-Armed": Chapter 265
    Section 26.
Firearm without FID Card, Possess": Chapter 269
    Section 10 (h).

And there would be additional charges and another indictment from the attorney general in Rhode
Island to come.

To everyone at the arraignment that day, it seemed

an impossible task to ever get an acquittal for the "Craigslist Killer." Cops had forensic evidence—the CSI-type that some pundits claim juries now demand because of the influence of watching the various *CSI* television shows. It had started to leak out to the best crime reporters that Boston Police had cell phone records and emails. They had the 9mm hidden in the hollowed-out copy of *Gray's Anatomy*, and bullets and shells from Julissa's murder scene which tests determined had been fired from that weapon. They had a positive identification of Markoff from Trisha Leffler, the prostitute robbed four days before Julissa's murder at a nearby Boston hotel. They also had clear surveillance photographs taken of Markoff as he left the hotel where Julissa was murdered, moments after it happened. They had the rolled-up panties hidden in Markoff's sweat socks under his bed, two pairs of which belonged to Trisha Leffler. They had the zip-ties and the duct tape. They had Markoff's fingerpints at the crime scenes. It certainly looked like a slam-dunk case.

But then again prosecutors and police thought the same thing about the Kyle Bryant case. That piece of shit confessed to being there. He had motive and means. And he got off. As far as a lot of cops were concerned, Salsberg had helped Bryant get away with a double homicide: the murder of his young, pregnant girlfriend and the slaying of his very own baby. If anyone had a shot at getting Philip Markoff off, the cops groused, it was John Salsberg.

Certainly Markoff's parents could not afford a "Super Lawyer" like Salsberg. But that would not be a concern. In Massachusetts, taxpayers pony up four times as much to pay for a suspect's defense than prosecutors are paid to put them away. Baby killer Neil Entwistle, who was convicted of murdering his wife Rachel and their baby Lillian Rose as they slept in their home in suburban Hopkinton, Massachusetts, on a freezing winter day in 2007, was assigned a criminal defense attorney who cost taxpayers more than $1 million. The Middlesex County assistant district attorney, who worked tirelessly to put the British-born baby killer in jail, earned roughly $60,000 a year. It was a maddening system, but as the refrain goes, "Only in Massachusetts," which had certainly earned its nickname, "Taxachusetts."

Salsberg would argue that his client was broke. In fact, he was more than broke. He was $130,000 in the red, loans he had expected to pay back with the six-figure income he would earn once he became a doctor. But the dreams of Philip becoming Dr. Markoff were completely scuttled now and a judge eventually ruled that Markoff was indigent and as such the taxpayers of Massachusetts would pick up the tab for his high-powered defense attorney. It was another blow to the cops. Their hard-earned paychecks would be lighter because of the staggering taxes they paid. Some of those monies would pick up the tab for Salsberg's salary. And the cost of private investigators. And forensic experts. And paralegals.

And every other damn thing that Salsberg needed to try to get Markoff off.

When the spectators in court that day finally got to hear Markoff speak, it was in a loud and confident voice, as if the mere act of saying the words with vigor would make people believe him.

"Do you understand the reading of the indictment?" the judge asked.

"Yes."

"How do you plead to the six counts in the indictment?"

"Not guilty."

As Markoff spoke, his parents stared at him. They looked stunned. Philip's words may have been uttered with confidence but his body refused to go along with the program. Philip was blinking uncontrollably, seemingly gasping for breath. His chest heaved up and down as if he was trying to suck in air to save his life, as if he were on the verge of hyperventilating.

Jon Markoff refused to look up at his brother. Jon scowled and appeared disgusted. *So much for Mr. Med School*, his expression seemed to say. Instead, he focused on his hand wrapped securely around his wife Deanna's hand. Hector Guzman sat in the front row and held his young daughter's hand. He was flanked by victim advocates from the Suffolk County District Attorney's Office, some of the hardest-working public employees in the state. The advocates see broken people nearly every day and Hector

Guzman—just like his ex-wife who had the sad task of identifying their daughter's bludgeoned, bullet-riddled body—was broken. His life would be forever damaged not only by the violence that claimed his daughter's life but by the secret profession she had hidden from her strict family who lived by the rules of decorum instilled in them in the Dominican Republic. His youngest daughter leaned her head into her dad's chest and sobbed. Her father pulled his only remaining child close, holding onto her for dear life. The details of the way Julissa died were brutal. She suffered a blow to her head so severe her skull was fractured. There were three close-range gunshot wounds that traveled through her body.

Assistant District Attorney Jennifer Hickman then stood up to reveal the litany of charges and the mountain of evidence they had gathered against Markoff.

She talked about the law enforcement agencies that had worked on the "Craigslist Killer" task force: Boston police, Boston University Police, Quincy police, the FBI, the attorney general's office, even the Secret Service. She talked about the forensic evidence gathered, in particular the cellular phone and the computer records that pointed toward Markoff's guilt. The ATF had traced the weapon already, a Springfield 9mm purchased, investigators later determined, during a time when Megan was in New Jersey planning their wedding. The weapon was bought from a gun store in Mason, New Hampshire, through the use of an identification that Markoff had apparently stolen from a friend of his from upstate New York. He then used that ID to obtain a fake driver's license which he used to buy the gun. Police had the fake ID and also recovered his fingerprints from the murder weapon's purchasing documents.

Police had also recovered disposable TracFones that Markoff had purchased, then used to contact Julissa Brisman and Trisha Leffler, as well as finding plastic ties identical to those used in the crimes against both women.

Given the overwhelming amount of evidence against Markoff, there was no amount of bail that would ensure he would return to court.

Just to make sure the judge understood, her bail demand, she reiterated, was "based on the forensic evidence from the crime scenes both at the Westin Hotel as well as the Copley Marriot Hotel. We received information, forensic evidence, not only from the crime scene but also from electronic and cellular communications, Internet communications, as well as surveillance video from two hotels, Your Honor."

Markoff did not look at her as she spoke. His father in the back row swallowed hard. The tops of his ears were flushed red.

"We know that it is the defendant before you, Philip Markoff, who on April 10, 2009, tied up a woman while she was at the Westin Hotel and that this is the defendant who, on April 14, 2009, bashed in the head of Julissa Brisman and shot her three times at close range.

"There's a commonality, Your Honor, between both of these two particular cases, that being that both of these women advertised services for masseuse on Craigslist, both of them were working out of hotels in downtown Boston, both women were bound or were attempted to be bound, both of the females were unarmed, and in the case of this particular incident, not only were these individuals bound but a gun was used as well.

"From the physical evidence that was obtained or recovered during the course of that particular hotel room it appears that Ms. Brisman put up a fight. She sustained blunt head trauma to her skull. She also received three gunshots at close range. Two of those gunshots were through and through. The third one was lodged in her left hip. One of the injuries, the bullet that went through Ms. Brisman's heart, according to the medical examiner, would've caused her death immediately. We know from video surveillance that the individual who killed Ms. Brisman walked calmly out of that Marriot Copley Hotel."

Philip Markoff stood in the defendant's box as Hickman spoke. He had completely zoned out. His eyes were blank. He had stopped blinking. He had stopped moving. At least, however, it didn't look like he was going to pass out anymore.

"During the course of the investigation," Hickman continued, "we've been able to track Internet information relative to an account used to make one of the appointments in this investigation. We were able to track the computer used to make up an email account to an IP address to Philip Markoff at an address in Quincy. We also know during the course of the investigation, Your Honor, that there was contact between this individual as well as with at least one of the victims. Your Honor, based on what the investigation was, a search warrant was executed last night at the defendant's home. Recovered during the execution of the search warrant was a semiautomatic firearm as well as ammunition, as well as items that were used or consistent with what were used to bind the victim in the Westin Hotel incident and were attempted to be used on Ms. Brisman during the incident at the Marriot Copley.

"Based on the violent nature of this case, Your Honor, as well as the brutal murder of an unarmed female, who appeared to have been fighting for her life as she was pulling off and trying to get away from this defendant, I ask that the defendant be held without bail on the murder complaint, Your Honor, and with a million-dollar cash bail on the kidnapping and armed robbery complaint."

Hickman would work the case with one of the best prosecutors in the city, a man with a long history of convictions, Ed Zabin. Zabin would become lead prosecutor on the case.

The judge nodded in agreement with the prosecutor. Markoff would be held without bail in connection with Julissa Brisman's murder, he ruled. The hearing was really a formality. No judge in his right mind was going to grant bail to the alleged Craigslist Killer. As another formality, bail was also set in connection with the attack on Leffler at $260,000.

As the arraignment came to a close, officials at Boston University had a hasty meeting. Administrators from the downtown Boston school had been inundated with requests for information from investigators from all of the agencies that Hickman had listed. They had also been bombarded with calls from reporters. School officials were not talking, except to offer "no comment." And that wasn't only for the press. They told investigators that they could not cooperate without a subpoena. As Markoff faced a judge, Boston University officials announced a decision of their own. The second-year medical student with decent grades had been suspended. That, of course, would prove to be the very least of Philip Markoff's problems at this point.

Markoff's lawyer was swarmed as he walked out of the courtroom. Reporters wanted answers or rather an explanation. Why would a handsome medical student with a gorgeous girlfriend and a promising future rob women at gunpoint for chump change? How did a guy without so much as an outstanding parking ticket, never mind criminal record, turn into a gun-toting murderer? Was there a history of mental problems? What?

Salsberg was a seasoned lawyer who knew how

to handle the media. He made a perfunctory claim of innocence. But he claimed he still needed to get up to speed on the case before he could comment further.

"Philip Markoff is not guilty of the charges. He has family support," Salsberg said. "I have nothing but words. I have not even received paperwork on this case. There is no proof of anything. We have to take a look at the evidence."

The questions from the reporters overlapped one another. TV reporters were looking for quick sound bites while the newspapers reporters tried to drag more substantial information out of Salsberg for what was sure to be tomorrow's front page story.

"Does he have a gambling problem?" a print reporter barked.

"I am not aware of a gambling problem," Salsberg answered in classic lawyerly fashion with the non-answer answer.

"How is your client holding up?" one TV reporter asked.

"Philip is bearing up. It's obviously a difficult time for anybody under these circumstances."

Then Salsberg hinted at a possible maneuver. "The jury pool has already been tainted," the defense attorney claimed. "Prosecutors have already poisoned the jury pool." With all this pretrial publicity, how could Philip possibly hope to get a fair trial in Boston, he asked.

Outside the courthouse a phalanx of wires from

satellite trucks used by television networks criss-
crossed the concrete and a microphone stand wob-
bled with the weight of more than a dozen boom
mikes. Reporters crouched to not block the shots
of the television cameras as Suffolk County District
Attorney Dan Conley emerged from the courthouse
to make a statement. If Conley was concerned that
what he said now might only fuel Salsberg's claim
that he and his office were trying to "poison the jury
pool," you'd never know it from his fiery comments
that followed.

"This was a brutal, vicious and savage crime. It
shows a real willingness to take advantage of women,"
Conley said. The cops who actually did the hard work
to arrest Markoff and build the case against him
stood back, out of view of the cameras.

"We will do everything we can to hold him accountable," Conley promised.

"The victim put up a pretty tough struggle and it
was in the context of that struggle that she lost her
life. She was a human being entitled to dignity and
respect."

Conley then said an autopsy showed that the fatal
bullet wound was the one that struck her heart. "It
went through-and-through," he said.

Then Conley said something that reporters seized
on, finally a nugget of new information.

"There is a possibility he has done this before,"
Conley said. "This is a very active and ongoing investigation."

Investigators were convinced there were others whom Markoff had victimized but because they were prostitutes, they didn't report his crimes.

"We're dealing with someone who is clearly clever," Conley said, "who certainly made efforts to hide himself from authorities by creating email addresses to contact these young women and also choosing women who were vulnerable, women who were perhaps living on life's margins, who perhaps would not contact authorities if they were victimized and this is the type of individual we are dealing with, someone who is willing to abuse women, to dominate them, to hurt them to get what he wants."

Conley once again reiterated the promise that women who believed they had encountered Markoff in the past would not be prosecuted for prostitution.

"Anyone who has been contacted by Philip Markoff . . . please let us know. I'm sure that these young women, if there are any others, would be worried about any possible prosecution on our end. We're not concerned about prosecuting these young women for offering massage services, or perhaps even other services. What I'm more concerned about, while I don't approve of that conduct, what I'm more concerned about is prosecuting Philip Markoff for any other incidents that he may have committed."

Then the Boston Police Department took what for them, a department that had only recently embraced the Internet as a potential crime-fighting tool, an extraordinary step.

In an effort to make a public plea to those Philip Markoff would have been most likely to victimized, the BPD took out its own "ad" in Craigslist's erotic services section.

> Were you attacked or robbed at a Boston-area hotel after placing an ad on Craigslist? If so, you may have information that could aid the investigation into the April 10 armed robbery of a woman at the Westin Copley Place Hotel and the April 14 murder of a woman at the Marriott Copley Place Hotel. Both victims were attacked by a prospective client who had contacted them through ads placed on Craigslist.

It was that ad that led at least one transvestite to contact police. And a simple Google search of one of Markoff's phone numbers listed under one of his pseudonyms would lead to a Craigslist ad that the medical school student apparently posted on his own. Oddly, it was under the head "Ebony Erotic Masseuse." The ad encouraged people to call the number supposedly as soon as possible because, it said, *taking my last appointment*. Cops were amazed at how much free time a medical student who was just months away from marriage was able to fit in for so many extracurricular sexual activities.

After Markoff's brief arraignment, he was en route to a place where he could likely give and receive as many man-on-man massages as he would like: the Nashua Street jail. If Philip Markoff was truly interested in experimenting with men, the Nashua Street jail might have been the perfect location. After a brief meeting with his new lawyer, Philip Markoff was transported by a deputy sheriff right back to the place that he would call home until his trial.

It was there that he would tell his family: "More is coming out."

13

"Yo, Craigslist!"

"Waddup, Murda Boy?"

Those were the taunts with which some of the jailbirds greeted the preppy and soft Philip Markoff as he was escorted into the booking area of the Suffolk County Jail.

In a holding cell, a deputy sheriff inventoried his property. There wasn't much, just the khaki pants and button-down shirt that his lawyer dressed him up in for his court appearance earlier that day. He had no jewelry to speak of. No tattoos or other distinguishing marks to note on the jail's "intake" forms. In fact, he was such a regular guy compared to the other "skels" in the joint that the sheriff who logged him into the system couldn't stop staring at him. He would later remark, "For jail, he was just so freakin' ordinary."

The sheriff snapped a picture of Philip Markoff that would become part of an identification card he would wear on his two-piece navy blue prison uniform. The picture shows Markoff staring down at his nose. The striped shirt he wore in court that day was rumpled. His face had broken out in angry red hives. His hair was a mess as if he had tugged at it in an attempt to pull it out. His lips pouted as if he was going to cry. There was no hint of the cool, calculating cold-blooded murderer prosecutors portrayed Markoff as earlier that morning at his arraignment. He looked like a teenager who was being bullied in a schoolyard rather than the "brutal savage" that Suffolk County District Attorney Dan Conley had described the Craigslist Killer suspect as being a few hours earlier.

After the inventory was taken he was handed a laundry bag. Inside were the standard-issue sheets and toiletries. Then he was sent to the "new man unit" which is classified as the 4-1 unit. There he was evaluated by a case worker for classification. He was also seen by a nurse who gave him a medical exam to check him for things such as sexually transmitted disease, lice and MRSA, methicillin-resistant *Staphylococcus aureus*, a staph infection that is highly resistant to antibiotics and quite prevalent in prisons. Once he was medically cleared, Markoff was sent to the "murder unit," which is known by the Suffolk County Sheriff's Department as the "6-2" high-factor unit.

On that day, April 21, 2009, Markoff wasn't the only notorious inmate in the cellblock. Christian Karl Gerhartsreiter didn't kill anyone but his case garnered far more media attention than 99.99 percent of the murders in Boston. Over the years the German-born con man, posing as Clark Rockefeller, had convinced a lot of prominent folks in New England's high society, including his millionaire wife, that he was a member of the Rockefeller family. Yeah, *those* Rockefellers. Gerhartsreiter had come to the United States as a teenager on a student visa as an exchange student in the late 1970s. By the time he snatched his seven-year-old daughter Reigh "Snooks" Boss from her mother's custody after a bitter divorce, Gerhartsreiter had also used the pseudonyms of Christopher Crowe and Christopher Chichester. His elaborate double and triple life, however, began to unravel with the kidnapping of his daughter on July 27, 2008, which took place on the fanciest block in New England on Marlboro Street during a supervised custody visit with his daughter. Rockefeller had paid a driver to ditch the social worker, violently, and took off, sparking an international manhunt. The subsequent investigation exposed "Rockefeller" as a lifelong con man and grafter, whose most recent role was posing as the "black sheep" scion of the famous dynasty. The forty-seven-year-old impostor charmed his way into Boston's privileged class. He lived around the corner from Massachusetts senator and former presidential candidate John Kerry and married a Harvard M.B.A. millionaire. He also wangled a job at the lush financial firm Kidder Peabody as an international salesman based on his phony name and a trumped-up resume. "Clark Rockefeller" showed off an extraordinary art collection to bolster his heritage claim. Of course, the art turned out to be fakes.

He was arrested in Baltimore six days after abducting his precocious daughter "Snooks." Gerhartsreiter had apparently established another secret life there where he was known as Charles "Chip" Smith and had kept a yacht moored in a local marina for the past nine years. In his short time on the lam, "Smith" was able to purchase a $450,000 condominium in an exclusive section of Baltimore. He used his ex-wife's money, of course.

When he was finally arrested on August 2, 2008, Gerhartsreiter was confronted with his past and with questions regarding skeletal remains dug up in a California backyard. That case involved the mysterious disappearance of a young couple, Jonathan and Linda Sohus, whom Gerhartsreiter rented a room from in San Marino. Though they suspect the bones found in the backyard of the home where Gerhartsreiter was staying were those of Jonathan Sohus, authorities weren't able to positively identify the bones as being Sohus because they had nothing to match them to. That investigation remains ongoing.

Rockefeller was in the "murder unit" not because of his crime but because the Woody Allen lookalike, a nebbishy weakling with thick, square, black-rimmed eyeglasses, needed to be separated from some of the rougher inmates for his own protection. His cell was not far from the newly accused murderer, the "Craigs-

list Killer." Another accused killer on the floor was
Jeffrey McGee, a man who killed his thirty-one-year-
old estranged wife, Christine, in November 2007 because he suspected her of having an affair with Sully
Erna, front man of the heavy metal rock band Godsmack. That case, too, had garnered national attention because McGee kidnapped his little boy after
he allegedly stabbed his wife to death with a knife
and razor two days after she partied with Godsmack
members.

After allegedly killing his wife, McGee, with his
son in tow, crashed into another car. Police who arrived at the scene reported that the boy told them,
"Daddy killed Mommy." Jeffrey McGee was charged
with domestic violence in 2003. Erna, the lead singer
of the multi-platinum heavy metal rock group,
admitted he hung out with McGee on several occasions before she was slain but denied any romantic
involvement with her. That didn't stop her husband
from accusing Christine of "fucking the rock star,"
which police believe led to the slaying.

McGee—one of those guys who in prison worked
hard to befriend other inmates and suck up to the
deputy sheriffs—was welcoming to Markoff when
he was on the unit. "What's up, Craigslist Killah . . . ?
Welcome to the jungle baby," McGee said to the preppie new guy in the murder unit. "How are you?"

If Markoff was in a talking mood, which he was
not, he would have replied, "Not too good."

Then there was Da-Ling Huang, another angry

reputed wife killer who had been charged five years earlier with cutting off his wife's breasts, then gutting her at their home in the Boston neighborhood of Allston. The victim was thirty-one years old and showed up with divorce papers when she was slain. He had been in the murder unit since 2005. He had become what deputy sheriffs call "a runner," an inmate who was so eager to please that they kept other prisoners in line. He would be convicted in 2010.

Markoff said nothing to any of his new compatriots. Even if he had wanted to spark a discussion with anyone it would have been difficult because he had been assigned to a "one-man" cell.

His lawyers, John Salsberg and Margaret Fox, visited that first day to check on their client and see if the proper steps had been taken to safeguard the vulnerable twenty-three-year-old medical school student.

"Keep in mind, he's a young man with no prior record, and he's being held at a jail," Salsberg told reporters as he was leaving. "It's difficult for anybody to be there, even if you're been there more than once. But I think he's bearing up."

The lawyers then left secure in the knowledge that Markoff was not in any danger, at least from the other inmates.

The same, however, could not be said about himself. In fact, Philip Markoff was not "bearing up," just the opposite.

In his one-man cell Philip Markoff would make

his first suicide attempt on April 23, two days after arriving at the jail. He was in a cell alone when he tied together the leather laces he had pulled out of his boat shoes—loafers very common with the country club set that Megan McAllister expected to someday belong to with her husband-to-be—and used the leather lanyard as a noose. He tied a loop around one of the cell bars and then pulled his neck tight against it. The leather broke, however, and the attempt failed. But a deputy sheriff on rounds immediately noted the welts on Markoff's neck and reported the apparent suicide attempt through prison channels.

Within minutes of the suicide attempt, news of Markoff trying to hang himself was reported by ABC News. He was immediately moved to the "suicide unit," the "5-5" unit, where he had a deputy sheriff assigned outside his cell around the clock. Despite the added attention, it would not be the last time Markoff attempted to end it all. But none of his attempts would be even remotely life-threatening. Privately, some of the guards wondered if Markoff really wanted to commit suicide or was just setting up some sort of insanity defense.

But in a matter of days Megan McAllister would visit her fiancé for the first time since she learned he was supposedly living a double life as the infamous Craigslist Killer. After that visit, Markoff would really have a reason to want to kill himself.

14

"Why not me? Why her?" Carmen Guzman screamed outside of the Ortiz Funeral Home in the Washington Heights section of Manhattan, New York, in her native Spanish.

"Por que, por que?" she wailed. *Why? Why?*

She then crumpled to her knees before her youngest daughter came to her aid. As they shuffled inside, daughter holding up mother, Carmen Guzman sobbed to her only surviving child saying in Spanish, "She was so young. She was just beginning to live her life."

Ortiz's was a funeral home that was popular among the city's growing Dominican population. Dominicans came from all New York City's five boroughs to the upper Manhattan funeral home to properly wake and bury their dead. But for the Guzmans it wasn't a long trip at all.

Julissa's parents, like many Hispanic and Irish families, had been priced out of their Hell's Kitchen neighborhood as the area gentrified and had since been pushed to Washington Heights, a predominantly Dominican section of upper Manhattan that traditionally is one of the poorest and most crime-ridden of New York City's neighborhoods. Carmen Guzman had settled on 170th Street, which was populated primarily by Dominicans and other Latinos but had also become a desirable block for yuppie couples who were trying to invest in Manhattan but could not afford to live alongside Sarah Jessica Parker—whose character in *Sex and the City* was Julissa Brisman's favorite—in the West Village or in a loft building near Robert DeNiro in Tribeca. It was changing, but Carmen Guzman was still old world and that's why she picked Ortiz Funeral Home.

On this afternoon, Ortiz Funeral Home had a labyrinthine line of mourners out front, many hanging their heads sadly that Julissa Brisman's young life had been snuffed out in such violent fashion. Some were visibly distraught, shaking with a combination of confusion, rage, grief and disbelief.

Jim Dyer was one of those mourners who were angry. He spoke for everyone who had taken umbrage at the description of Julissa Brisman as a "hooker."

"She was not a hooker," the slightly-built twenty-four-year-old said. "She was fragile, delicate, warm."

A neighbor of Julissa's on the lower East Side echoed that. "It's a bunch of lies they're saying about her," Edna Cales told reporters. "She was a good girl."

One of the founding members of the 1970s rock sensation Blondie had met Julissa Brisman at City

College. Keyboardist Jimmy Destri, who also had his battles with alcohol and drug addiction, was contacted by the *New York Daily News* and had nothing but kind words for his slain classmate. "This is a girl who was trying to turn her life around. She had her demons and she dealt with them. We all had backgrounds but she was a really nice kid. She was sweet. I want people to know that she was more than 'the masseuse.'"

Over and over again mourners told reporters that Julissa Brisman "was not a hooker." They talked about her sweet nature and her easy smile. They referred to her love of her dog Coco Chanel and her dedication to friends and family. "She was not a hooker. She was NOT a hooker," Edna Cales protested to a NBC News cameraman. "She was a good person. She was always there for all of her friends."

As Carmen and Hector Guzman wept over the death of their daughter at the funeral home, and held a private Mass for her the following morning that was conducted in Spanish without the prying eyes of the press who were asked not to attend, a newspaper in upstate New York carried a story about a native son gone bad.

"The residents of the city of Sherrill are in shock and disbelief as one of their own has been charged with a horrific crime five hours away from this tightly-knit community," the *Oneida Dispatch*'s story started.

What happened was clearly big news in rural upstate New York and had ripped apart their small town. The horrific crime had obviously stunned the people who loved Julissa Brisman and, judging from the line outside Ortiz's that day, people from all over New York. And judging from the tone of the story in Markoff's hometown paper which was published two hundred and seventy miles north, the good people of small-town Sherill were equally as shocked and perhaps filled with a little guilt that one of their very own was the notorious Craigslist Killer. School officials tripped over themselves to talk about what a great student Phil Markoff had been. Markoff's family went into hiding, staying with friends rather than facing the onslaught of reporters and the questioning looks from their lifelong neighbors.

And back in Boston, the citizenry was still struggling to come to terms with how Markoff, drawn to their city like tens of thousands of other young people to attend their world-renowned colleges and universities, could morph from medical school student to murderer like some modern-day Jekyll and Hyde. But the impact the Craigslist Killer carried far beyond those three cities; it carried across the nation.

On Julissa Brisman's Facebook page her sober friends, compatriots in the battle to stay sober, began to post musings about her. It was clear to those in the twelve-step programs who had encountered Brisman that she would have made a very good drug and alcohol counselor. She was "warm" as one friend had described her. More importantly, she was approachable, which was an indispensable trait when dealing with people who were walking into their first meeting, shaking and scared and unsure they could go through with it.

Beth: I loved you when you were a crazy brazen blonde, I loved you as a stunning studios brunette in AA. I'm so sorry this happened to you.

Annie: I remember meeting you when I had just three days and was shaking like a leaf. You came up to me and we clicked right away. You were sooo sweet. Rest in peace beautiful. You are missed and loved and in everyone's prayers.

Sabrina: I will miss your positivity and your adorable comments, and every time I think of you just makes me so damn mad at that bastard.

Max: I'll do my best to make sure that motherfucker who shot you gets his balls cut off and stuffed down his throat.

Another attractive woman whose face had been splashed on the front pages of the New York tabloid newspapers was also devastated by Julissa Brisman's murder. Her name was Kristin Davis, also known as the Manhattan Madam, after then-New York governor, Eliot Spitzer, was forced to resign after being caught up soliciting prostitutes from the Emperors Club VIP escort services where he was unveiled as the infamous "Client No. 9."

After Spitzer stepped down in disgrace, Kristin Davis came forward to say that he had also used her Wicked Models escort service in the past. In her book, *Manhattan Madam*, she described Spitzer as "rough" and accused the disgraced governor and former top lawman as the attorney general of New York of being a "weasel" about wearing a condom with her girls and had proclivities that included rough sex and toys. She also described her business relationship with Brisman, who worked for her, to the *New York Daily News*. "She was a good kid, but kind of a nightmare," Davis told *The News*. "She had a bad drinking problem. We rescued her a couple of times from a bar where she hung out when she was supposed to be working.

"I kept giving her second chances," the madam added. "She'd come back and promise she was sober."

Davis insisted that over the year and a half she booked dates for Brisman, the stunning model used the name "Stacey." Stacey only offered only sensual body rubs and wasn't selling sex, said the madam. "She didn't do escorting."

At the time of that interview, Davis, a busty, broad-shouldered blonde, had been placed on probation for five years after pleading guilty to promoting prostitution and serving three months in jail. She was not surprised to hear that her former employee had been targeted by posting a Craigslist ad. Such Craigslist-fueled violence is no surprise to Davis, who said that several young women who offer sexual services online have come to her with tales of horror.

Some online stalkers even impersonate cops and force the women to hand over their cash or face "arrest," the former madam said. "If they hit the girls at the right time," Davis said, "they may come away with a thousand dollars." That's exactly what prosecutors and police worried about with the Craigslist Killer. There were sixteen pairs of panties found in the Markoff home. Four pairs of panties were found bundled into socks under his bed. He was so comfortable in the Leffler robbery that cops were convinced that he had done it before.

None of that mattered to Carmen Guzman. All she knew was that her daughter was dead. She didn't read the stories about how Julissa worked for the notorious Manhattan Madam. She wanted to forget how her daughter died at the hands of a "customer," a "stranger," just as it looked like she was finally starting to pull her life together. Even the Manhattan Madam acknowledged that her friend had gotten sober. "She was doing good in life. She deserved better than what happened to her."

Meanwhile, Facebook would continue to play a role in the Craigslist Killer case. One of Markoff's either myopic or contrarian high school buddies set up a "Phil Markoff Is Innocent Until Proven Guilty" Facebook page. It read: "Rally against the media who is quick to place blame, against the culture that has forgotten that people like Phil are suspects, not killers. . . . His guilt or innocent [*sic*] is really not the reason for this group—the reason for this group is encouraging and reminding the American public how our legal system works and to not let them get sucked into the media coverage that is quick to forget the very basis of due process and a fair trial before one's peers."

One man was apparently not so convinced of Phil Markoff's innocence, however: himself.

Philip Markoff had some ties to sever and he would do it in the visitors' room at the Nashua Street jail.

15

The date was April 24, 2009. Susan Haynes and Richard Markoff had now been in Boston for three very long days. If it seemed to them that they were under constant media surveillance, it's because they were. When they were able to finally shake the reporters, they still couldn't look at a newspaper or turn on the radio or TV and not hear about their son, the alleged Craigslist Killer. If they were able to completely tune out all the media, it didn't matter because wherever they, whomever they encountered, it was all anyone in Boston was talking about; the store-owner at the corner grocery, the cabbie, the hotel bellboy, their waiter, whoever.

Hell, even when they were completely by themselves, how could Philip Markoff's parents think about anything other than the fact that their progeny, the one who was supposed to a doctor, a success story, was now in a jail accused of embarking on a murderous weeklong, gambling-fueled crime spree?

The divorced couple's nerves were frayed. The pain that Susan Haynes felt was etched on her face. Reporters had followed them around screaming questions, demanding answers. She would respond with a stone-cold look. Her ex-husband was nagging her. Her son Jon was walking around in a simmering rage. They couldn't leave town until they first saw Philip, and now the Suffolk County Jail would not allow any visitors because Philip was on suicide watch after attempting to hang himself.

John Salsberg would not confirm that his client had in fact tried to kill himself but did say that he had "grave concerns with the psychological state of his client."

Salsberg walked past a throng of reporters who had camped outside the Suffolk County Jail on Nashua Street, which many Bostonians still considered its "new" location. The old Suffolk County Jail had been located on Charles Street, a short walk from the old Boston Garden. The "Charles Street jail," as everyone called it, was built around 1840 and had more than its share of famous prisoners over the years, including Boston mayor James Michael Curley, the "Rascal King," who did five months in the jail in 1947 on mail fraud charges; Sacco and Vanzetti, the Italian-born anarchists who many believe were wrongly executed for a 1920 armed robbery and murder of a pay clerk; Malcolm X, when he was a small-time hood still named Malcolm "Big Red" Little; and the Boston Strangler, to name a few.

In 1973, a federal judge ruled that the rights of the prisoners in the antiquated jail were being violated because of severe overcrowding. So Boston officials built a new jail to rectify the situation . . . seventeen years later. Amusingly, developers have since sunk $150 million into renovating the gothic slammer and it's now one of Boston's hottest luxury hotels, with the tongue-in-cheek name of The Liberty. In fact, the trendy bar in The Liberty, with the equally tongue-in-cheek name of The Alibi, was the preferred watering hole for many of the reporters covering the Craigslist Killer case.

Anyway, on April 24, Markoff's parents, his brother and sister-in-law were finally granted a visit with Philip. The day happened to fall on what would have been Julissa Brisman's twenty-sixth birthday.

As the group approached the reporters standing watch pounced.

They screeched out questions.

"Do you think your son is guilty?"

"Why did your son try to kill himself?"

"Are you in touch with Megan?"

"Is your son the Craigslist Killer?"

"Do you blame yourselves?"

"What is your son's state of mind?"

"Has he said anything to you?"

"Where is his fiancée?"

The questions hit the Markoff family like a frying pan to the face. Susan Haynes actually cringed at the mention of Megan's name. She had never spent a lot of time with her son's fiancée; in fact they had merely had one dinner together near the holidays the year before. Sure, she was happy that her son had met such a classy girl, a woman who clearly had the capacity to take care of Philip. But Philip was a young man. He was going to be a doctor. No one could blame Susan Haynes for thinking that her son was too young to be married, no matter how sweet and pretty his fiancée was. No matter that her family thought Megan was too good for Philip.

Philip's attorney John Salsberg tried to shield the Markoffs from the rabid reporters as best he could. He was used to it. Salsberg was the type of guy who had a penchant for taking on media cases. He was constantly barraged by reporters outside the arraignments for his notorious clients. The reporters had been standing outside for hours, gossiping about the trade, bitching about their bosses, drinking coffee and generally trying to fend off boredom. To see the Markoff clan walk up to the jailhouse entrance was the most action they had seen in days and they understandably tried to take full advantage of it. And Salsberg, understandably, tried to run interference. After all, being a defense attorney on a high-publicity case wasn't all about what you did in the courtroom.

"In a difficult time, having people from the press put microphones in your face is not something anyone wants," Salsberg told the reporters. At least one reporter scoffed at his remarks, saying out loud to a cameraman: "Yeah, unless you are a press-hungry defense attorney who represents women-killers."

Salsberg went on, trying to squelch the assumption that had spread among the reporters that Markoff's family did not support him because they had waited three days to show up at the Nashua Street jail.

"He couldn't have any visitors until he was classified by the jail. And my understanding was that the first day they could come was today. . . . I would just say that everybody who is incarcerated here is in a difficult situation and I wouldn't say that he is an exception to anyone else here. This is difficult. They really request privacy. They ask that any questions you have, you ask of me.

"They love their son very much and are supportive of him. That's what they would say if they were speaking to you." But they weren't.

Because Markoff was still on suicide watch the meeting was monitored by deputy sheriffs, one of whom would later tell his colleagues that it was "strangely cold."

"They all just kind of stared at each other. His mother teared up when she saw the marks on his neck," a source at the Nashua Street jail would later say. "It was odd. Like they were all strangers to one another."

But it was a meeting with Jon Markoff, Philip's brother, that would provide the most insight into the mind of the alleged killer.

Dave Wedge of the *Boston Herald* got a call from

inside the jail. Apparently there was a very emotional meeting between the siblings. Markoff began to weep. Jon was uncomfortable.

"Forget about me. . . . There is more coming out," Markoff said through tears. "Move to California."

But even in California the case had garnered notoriety. Especially when Megan McAllister, the fiancée who had initially steadfastly stood by her man, went to the jail to break off their engagement.

There was only so much that Megan McAllister could take. She wanted to stick by Philip. She loved him. But a lot had come out since she contacted the media on the day Philip was arrested, April 20, declaring his innocence and saying Philip "couldn't hurt a fly."

She had spent the past eight long days holed up in her parents' home in Little Silver, New Jersey, hiding from the world. But there was no way from keeping herself isolated from the flood of information that kept pouring out about her fiancé, about the Craigslist Killer.

She had to hire an attorney, a spokesman. He was famous in media circles, a frequent contributor to the network news. His name was Robert "Bob" Honecker. He was a New Jersey "Super Lawyer" and was very savvy in dealing with the media.

On April 27 Honecker held a press conference outside the home of Megan's parents to read a short statement and announce that Megan wouldn't be commenting publicly any further on the matter.

"It's my intent to fully cooperate with my finacé's attorney as well as the Suffolk County District Attorney's Office as they both continue their investigations," her statement read. "I can only tell them what I know and what is the truth."

In an astonishing turn of events, the woman who, unsolicited, contacted several television stations, newspapers and magazines on the day her fiancé was arrested to declare his innocence has not publicity uttered another word about the case since. Nor is she likely to.

If her unwavering loyalty to Philip Markoff has since started to waver somewhat, it's understandable.

For instance, imagine hearing a report about *your* fiancé like the one from the *Today* show on what *hers* had been up to behind her back.

NBC reporter Jeff Rossen told a national audience—which of course included Megan's friends and family in New Jersey, her former classmates at SUNY Albany, everyone she knew—that Phil Markoff had been corresponding with another guy in 2008. That's right. A guy. Lascivious, erotic emails that Phil had sent to another man whose identity was shadowed on the air, a man who had posted a Craigslist ad in the casual encounters section under M4T—a term that translated into men looking for transsexuals, transvestites and transgendered. The email exchanges were flashed on television, with Markoff using the term of endearment "babe." Babe. The same term of endearment that he used when he smiled at Megan or made her breakfast in bed. Markoff's emails went this way:

"I am a 22/y/o grad student, 6'3", 205, good build, blond, blue eyes . . . what are you into and what are your stats? What are you doing tonight."

It was not out of the ordinary for casual encounters ads on Craigslist to mean exactly that. A quick hookup in the steam room of a fancy downtown Boston gym; a knock at the door of a stranger's home and then raunchy, anonymous sex. It happened all the time. But what was unusual about Markoff's posting is that he used his full name and included pictures of himself that showed his face. It was an extraordinarily reckless behavior for a man who not only had just become engaged but also had recently been accepted into medical school. It got worse. Markoff even included pictures of him pleasuring himself. The exchanges went on for months with the last one sent in January 2009, four months before Julissa Brisman was murdered.

"He seemed like a great guy," the transvestite told NBC News. "He was very cute. I was taken by his looks."

Rossen asked the transvestite how he thought Markoff's fiancé would take the latest twist in the sex saga that was being unveiled in her fiancé's life. He was sympathetic.

"It would be tough for anyone to hear that their fiancé is saying he's single and looking for sex online anonymously with men, men who dress up as women, with transsexuals, with anyone he could get online," he said. "This person [Markoff] was trolling Craigslist like a Monopoly game."

No one could know for sure what Megan McAllister was thinking. She wasn't talking to anyone except for her parents and three older brothers. But she definitely was no longer going to be Phil Markoff's most ardent supporter. In fact, she finally had had enough of ridicule, the humiliation. Honecker hinted that she was backing off saying, "Obviously what's been put forth in the media and by authorities is subject to further investigation and it's going to be tested at some point in a court of law." Honecker continued, "The family and friends of Megan are supporting her tremendously. I think they realize that if some of these allegations were, in fact, true this may have been a situation where she was fortunate."

To make matters even more embarrassing for McAllister, her fiancé's attorney had filed a brief with the courts requesting that the Massachusetts taxpayers pay for his client's defense. He was indigent, the argument went, and owed creditors more than $130,000. Most of the money was from student loans. But it was still humiliating. Megan had always been led to believe that they were financially secure. She never worried about money and Philip was always flashing a wad of cash whenever they went anywhere. Not only was he being accused of murder, he was flat broke.

More is coming out, Markoff had told his brother. He wasn't kidding.

Megan's lawyer nailed it. If everything that had come out about the man she thought was the love of her life then she was better off taking the advice Philip passed on to his family: "Forget about me."

But it was something that had to be said in person. A phone call or letter wouldn't do.

On April 29, Megan looked stunning and stunned as she walked into the Nashua Street jail.

Had Philip somehow had access to the *Star-Ledger,* New Jersey's largest daily newspaper, he would have been tipped off to what was coming.

A story that ran in the *Star-Ledger* the day before Megan visited Markoff in the Nashua Street jail read, "The fiancée of a medical student accused of killing a masseuse he met through Craigslist said Monday she still loves him, but the band hired to perform at their scheduled August wedding in New Jersey said it's been told it won't be needed."

The story stated that "it was unclear whether cancellation of the band means the wedding is delayed or off."

The BStreetBand, a Bruce Springsteen tribute band, had been scheduled to play at the New Jersey oceanside wedding August 14. But now, the band was available for another gig on that date, according to its website. "Due to circumstances beyond our control, this date is now available to book," says a blurb on its performance schedule.

William Forte, the keyboardist and owner of the BStreetBand, said a relative of McAllister called him and said "that as of right now, there is no way they will be able to have the August 14 wedding date."

Forte said he planned to return the couple's $500 deposit.

"Under the circumstances, I would never hold them to the contract," Forte said.

As she entered the jail that day, Megan hid her eyes, red from crying, behind dark sunglasses. She looked sleek and busty in a black short-sleeved sweater and black slacks with heels. By her side was her mother, dressed smartly in a tan blazer and a white blouse. Both women looked nervous, frazzled and preoccupied, especially Megan. How could she not be nervous and preoccupied when in a few minutes she'd be telling a man she once loved so unconditionally they were through. Reporters noted that she was not wearing her engagement ring. Why would she? It was a slap in the face to consider what the ring represented. He gave it to her while calling a transvestite "babe." He took pictures of himself masturbating and shared them with the world online. The humiliation was too much.

The visit was a short one, the message simple. Megan McAllister broke off the engagement. She told Philip she would probably never see him again.

The breakup took roughly twenty-five minutes. A sheriff would later say that Philip Markoff didn't say much. He didn't plead with her to reconsider. He didn't proclaim his innocence. He stared at her and muttered: "I'm sorry."

McAllister had already dismantled their wedding website on April 23, the same day that her fiancé tried to kill himself with his leather shoelaces. She was not wearing her diamond engagement ring when she went in. But it was not as if she could have handed it back to him. It would have just been taken by the security staff inside the prison anyway. Philip looked awful that day. The prison officials no longer trusted him with the normal prison jumper or shoes and especially not shoelaces.

When he met with Megan, he had been given what law enforcement officials called a "Ferguson Safety Blanket"—a long, heavily padded, sleeveless robe that, according to the company's website, has "no loops, ties, ribbing or edging to be torn off into strips" and also "no hard fasteners to be swallowed or filed into weapons." In other words, only the truly dangerous, either to themselves or others, are forced to wear these smocks. It was a precaution. The deputy sheriffs did not want him ripping up the two-piece jail ensemble to fashion into a noose or a ligature. There was no ripping at the Ferguson blanket. But at least it was better than the flimsy paper hospital gown he had been wearing when he had to see his parents, the kind you tie in the back that never really close all the way.

A witness to the meeting said that Megan also did not cry. Instead she sat next to her mother and both women remained stoic. Philip did not say much. Just shook his head sadly and whispered, "I'm sorry." That was enough. Megan stood up, spun around and left. She stormed past the awaiting reporters without saying a word. Honecker would answer questions from the media instead.

"They had a candid, frank discussion," though he didn't know specifics of what was said. He said his client had been distraught about coming to Boston to meet with Markoff.

"She's done it now, and I think she feels good about coming up and seeing him," Honecker said. "But now it's time to move on with other things in her life."

When asked about McAllister's demeanor after meeting with Markoff, Honecker said she was understandably emotional. She had planned on marrying this man, having kids, building a future, growing old together, the whole nine yards. She wanted the pink kitchen and the matching luggage and the Vera Wang china. She wanted to be the wife of a doctor and now she had become a national laughingstock; a symbol of a woman who was so desperate for the fairy-tale wedding that she failed to notice her man stashing stolen underwear under their bed and secreting a gun in a medical textbook. She failed to notice that a woman he stood accused of killing had left scratch marks on his body. She failed to notice that he had been exchanging sexually explicit emails and photographs with men and women alike.

She had been accepted to medical school in St. Kitts but had initially abandoned any thought of moving to the Caribbean because she wanted to focus on her upcoming marriage and support the man she loved. But as they say, things change. Now instead of planning on being the wife of a doctor, she had decided to rededicate herself to her original plans. She was planning on attending medical school in St. Kitts again. Maybe there they won't have heard about the Craigslist Killer.

"But she's a very bright, articulate young woman, and she's beginning to understand that she has to find strength from those around her and from those who support her," Honecker said. "I think this was a big step for her to realize the seriousness of the charges her fiancé faces. And also that she has to get on and take care of herself and the rest of her life."

Honecker didn't know if McAllister would meet with Markoff, again, ever. He said she would immediately return to New Jersey after leaving the Nashua Street jail. He did fudge that detail a bit.

Neighbors at the apartment where Markoff and McAllister had lived noted that on that very day Megan bid Philip farewell there was a U-Haul truck outside the building. Megan McAllister had been given permission by the Boston Police Department to remove her belongings. Her parents were helping her carry out boxes and furniture. They wanted to wipe out any sign of her life with Philip.

"She's going to take up her life with her friends

and her family in New Jersey," Honecker said. He added if the district attorney doesn't request a meeting with McAllister, "I don't expect her to return in the near future."

Honecker said so far the Suffolk County district attorney, Dan Conley, had not requested a meeting with McAllister or asked her to testify before a grand jury. That would be short-lived. Of course the district attorney wanted her to testify before the grand jury, which eventually indicted Philip Markoff.

On April 30, 2009—the day after Megan McAllister told him she would never see him again—Philip Markoff tried to kill himself again. This time he sharpened a metal spoon against the concrete in his cell until he got a reasonably sharp edge. He raked it across his wrists, back and forth, back and forth. He managed to draw blood, but that was about it.

Once again Philip Markoff was back in the medical ward. Alone. Wearing nothing but a suicide blanket.

16

As April 2009 turned to May, Philip Markoff seemingly had nothing left to live for. He was locked down in a one-man cell inside the Suffolk County Jail, forced to dress either in a tissue-paper-like hospital gown, or a special padded robe that was designed specifically so he could not twist or rip it into a rope and hang himself. As the accused Craigslist Killer, he was, by far, the most notorious accused criminal in all of New England and New York, at that point, and maybe in the entire country. The evidence pointing toward his guilt for a laundry list of charges, including murder, kidnapping and armed robbery, during a seven-day crime spree was formidable and ever-growing. In addition to his alleged criminal acts, the media had uncovered, and subsequently reported with glee, Markoff's hithertofore secret seeming fetishes: transvestites and cross-dressing. He had pissed a promising medical career down the drain and publicly humiliated himself, his family and his fiancée . . . or rather his former fiancée, who understandably finally dumped him on April 29.

Things were going so bad for Markoff, he couldn't even kill himself. Twice he tried, twice he failed. There would be a third attempt. Shoelaces of his boat shoes broke the first time and a spoon he'd sharpened left only superficial slice marks on his wrist. Now that he was placed on "suicide watch," the authorities were doing everything in their power not to let Markoff kill himself. Even if suicide would be the quickest, easiest solution for everyone involved, the system now demanded that Markoff be kept alive so that he could be dragged into court, tried, and if convicted, sent to a prison for the rest of his life.

And life without parole was what Markoff faced if convicted of tying up and robbing a prostitute named Trisha Leffler on April 10 in the Westin Copley hotel in Boston and then beating and fatally shooting Julissa Brisman, a twenty-five-year-old sensual masseuse, four days later down the street at the Marriott Copley.

So more than a few Boston cops and prosecutors had to roll their eyes when Rhode Island attorney general Patrick C. Lynch called a press conference for May 4.

The attorney general in Rhode Island wanted a piece of this case even if their jurisdiction—their "juice," as cops called it—was pretty minimal. The

Craigslist Killer had tried to rob a prostitute in a Warwick hotel on April 16, 2009, two days after Julissa was murdered, but the plan went awry when the hooker's husband barged in. Patrick Lynch knew all too well they wouldn't be able to extradite Markoff until the more serious Boston cases were resolved. He also knew that their victim, Cynthia Melton, didn't want to cooperate. In fact, as he spoke to the assembled press she was "in the wind," as cops say, vanished.

Of course, Rhode Island authorities were legally bound to pursue the case, they couldn't just forget about it. But having a press conference to announce an arrest warrant had been issued for a guy who was already in jail, wearing a Ferguson Safety Blanket no less, smacked a bit of grandstanding. Politics.

Lynch certainly wasn't the first elected official who would be guilty of trying to get his face on the nightly news. And, for what it's worth, it worked. Reporters who had covered every nugget of the case up until then were not going to pass up on another story about the Craigslist Killer, no matter how inconsequential. The room at the Warwick Police Department's headquarters where the media gathered was packed. Boston reporters had driven nearly an hour. New York tabloid reporters from the *Daily News* and the *Post* had been staying in Boston since Markoff had been pinched driving south to Foxwoods on April 20.

Flanked by Warwick police chief Stephen M.

McCartney, Lynch approached the podium and the bouquet of microphones set up on it while cameras clicked away.

"After a three-week investigation, we have secured a warrant for the arrest of Philip Markoff, who resides at 8 Highpoint Circle in Quincy, Massachusetts. Markoff, a second-year medical student at Boston University, will be charged with the April 16 late-night attempted robbery that occurred in the Holiday Inn Express hotel, located at 901 Jefferson Boulevard in Warwick.

"Markoff will face one count of assault with intent to commit robbery; one count of assault with a dangerous weapon; one count of possession of a handgun without a license; and one count of using a firearm while committing a crime of violence.

"The first two counts carry twenty-year maximum penalties. The second two charges carry maximum penalties of ten years. If convicted of the last count, Markoff could face ten years to be imposed consecutively, as opposed to concurrently, with any other sentence he could face in this case."

Lynch knew that authorities in Massachusetts might be scoffing at the dog and pony show he was putting on for the press. So he assuaged their irritation by acknowledging he was basically powerless to do anything to bring Markoff to justice until the cases in Boston had been resolved.

"Because the defendant has been charged with murder, robbery and other crimes in Boston, he will be in the custody of the Commonwealth until District Attorney [Dan] Conley has finished prosecuting his office's cases against him, and, if Markoff is ultimately convicted in Boston, until he is sentenced," Lynch said. "Although the filing of a warrant for Markoff's arrest might seem academic because he is being held at that Nashua Street jail, it's an important milestone for our case nonetheless.

"We will continue to cooperate with D.A. Conley's office and the Boston police. We will file a detainer with the Massachusetts corrections authorities to ensure they know that Markoff is a wanted man here in Rhode Island," he said, adding, unnecessarily of course, "And we will simply wait our turn to prosecute."

Of course, Lynch didn't mention that if Markoff was convicted of the Boston charges and thus sentenced to life in prison, there was no way in hell they would waste time and taxpayers' money by pursuing an attempted murder charge with an uncooperative prostitute witness. But Rhode Island is a small, relatively crime-free state. And you can't begrudge an elected official like Lynch his media face time since he doesn't get too much of it. He ended by praising the police work on the case.

"There has been intense media coverage of this defendant and his alleged crimes. Rhode Island's court rules, however, are very clear about the lawyers who are involved in a case not making any comments that could have a prejudicial effect on the case," he said. "The one thing I am very comfortable saying, though, is that people of Warwick and all of Rhode Island can and should be proud of the work of the Warwick Police Department in this case, because it has been exemplary."

Though it was an obvious attention-grab by Lynch, there was no denying that the investigative work by the Warwick cops and Rhode Island State Police was exemplary. But it should have been Suffolk County district attorney Dan Conley and Boston police commissioner Ed Davis thanking them, not Lynch.

Rhode Island investigators had found important evidence that might be able to help Dan Conley with his case, while the chances of Markoff ever going to trial in Rhode Island are very slim. Conley could scoff all he wanted at Lynch getting his face time in this national story but the truth remained that the Warwick cops sprang into action the minute they arrived at the Holiday Inn. They spotted the zip-tie restraints and heard the description of the perpetrator and knew right away that this case could be connected to the Craigslist Killer murder they had been hearing about up north for the past two days, ever since Julissa Brisman was discovered murdered. Because the investigators were "raised up" as they say, or on high alert, because of the fact that the robbery sounded like the work of the Craigslist Killer, they also thoroughly interviewed Cynthia Melton. That's not something that given the circumstances, an attempted robbery of a prostitute in a rundown hotel, cops would have automatically done. What Melton told them was she thought that Markoff stole her panties, something that might come out at Markoff's trials in Boston. Of course, at the press conference Colonel McCartney would not provide details on what evidence his investigators had gathered. All he would say is: "We got a clue from the complaining witness that there may be some connection."

That would not be the only clue linking Markoff to the Warwick robbery. He was caught on surveillance tape at the nearby Walmart buying a baseball cap in a very half-hearted attempt to conceal his identity. His cell phone number had pinged off nearby cell towers. And he left his fingerprints in the stairwell that he used to run from the victim's husband.

Lynch was asked whether the victim's reluctance would be a factor when he tried to prosecute Phil Markoff. He would only say that Melton had "helped enough."

"The victim has been responsive," Lynch said. "The victim has been cooperative enough."

Enough to base an entire, expensive prosecution on years down the road, especially if a conviction would mean only adding symbolic years to a life-without-parole sentence? It seems highly unlikely. But on May 4, 2009, before a national media, Lynch promised that would someday be the case no matter what happened to Markoff on his Boston cases.

"He will be brought to justice," Lynch assured the assembled reporters. "But it may take some time to bring him formally to Rhode Island."

Though most of his press conference was fluff, Lynch, almost as an aside, mentioned that he was none too happy with the response of Craigslist officials. "The guy from Craigslist was on TV," Lynch said, alluding to an interview with a company official that aired the previous week. "He said it was only one incident. I think it was totally irresponsible. It was a murder."

The *Boston Globe* reported that Lynch, who was then the president of the National Association of Attorneys General, said he has worked with law enforcement officials across the country to get Internet companies, including Craigslist, to be "better corporate citizens." He said they had to make more of an effort to improve online safety such as requiring those who place erotic ads to use "traceable credit cards" but added that more needs to be done.

The tone of the article made it seem possibly that Lynch might look into bringing charges against the corporate giants for acting like corporate pimps.

"This case is a very stark, difficult, horrific reminder that there are predators out there," Lynch admonished that day. "Corporate citizens have to step up and take a role in keeping the Internet safe."

Apparently buoyed that his aside received prominent play in the stories, Lynch put out a press release two days later; "AG Lynch urges Craigslist to 'pick up the pace' in eliminating 'erotic services' ads."

The headline was promising as was the first few words of the statement. "Craigslist needs to pick up the pace in removing its 'erotic services' ads" or risk facing . . ." But midsentence Lynch's resolve fizzled, ". . . continued pressure from his peers nationally."

Lynch was referring to Craigslist CEO Jim Buckmaster and "continued pressure from his peers" was as tough as Lynch was willing to get.

The press release continued along impotently for the rest of the page. Lynch, it said, "stopped short, however, of threatening to prosecute Craigslist, stating: 'I am convinced that cooperating will bring better results, and more quickly, than confrontation.'"

The remainder sounded almost conciliatory. The most salient part read like someone in his office did the research and came back with the bad news that there was no way to hold Craigslist legally liable for Markoff's actions.

"In the same way that Craigslist needs to balance its profits with its responsibilities, we, as prosecutors, need to balance our powers and responsibilities. I'm not sure that a web site would be considered liable, or could be prosecuted, for content posted by its users. I think that building on the relationship and agreement we have already forged with Craigslist will help make the Internet safer, faster than taking Craigslist and other websites to court."

In the coming months, attorneys general from other states would vehemently voice their opposition to Lynch's stance of negotiation over prosecution. They would make noise about making Craigslist more accountable. But while prostitution was one issue, murder, which was causing this outcry, was quite a different story. Craigslist's officials could do no more to stop some psycho bent on using Craigslist to commit criminal acts on those advertising with their site than the phone company could do to stop someone who robs a delivery person by calling in an order.

Yet because Philip Markoff had been branded the "Craigslist Killer" and the case was receiving enormous media attention, the politicians were screaming for action. To make matters worse for Craigslist's officials, Markoff's case had caused reporters to start digging around for other crimes committed through the website and they soon discovered that Philip Markoff wasn't the first to use Craigslist to commit crimes, not by a long shot. In fact, Philip Markoff wasn't even the first "Craigslist Killer."

17

Though Philip Markoff has been dubbed the "Craigslist Killer," he is certainly not the only person who became notorious for using Craigslist in an alleged crime.

Three and a half weeks before authorities say that Markoff murdered a sensual masseuse named Julissa Brisman in a downtown Boston hotel, a radio reporter was killed by a teen he met on Craigslist. Twelve days before Markoff allegedly killed Julissa, another man also dubbed the "Craigslist Killer," but in a much smaller media market, was sentenced to life in prison for murdering a young woman he'd lured to his home in Minnesota by posting a phony ad for a babysitter. Then less than two months after Julissa's slaying, a pregnant woman in Oregon was murdered after answering yet another Craigslist ad from someone purporting to be selling baby clothes.

Murder was certainly the last thing Craig Newmark envisioned that his list would help facilitate when he started emailing his friends and work acquaintances with events that were going on in and around the San Francisco area in the mid 1990s.

An unassuming man, Newmark sports a goatee and many of his publicity photographs show him bespectacled and wearing a black scaly cap on top of shorn black hair. In 1995, while working as an IT technician for the discount investment firm of Charles Schwab in San Francisco, Newmark began what started as a "fun side project," an email distribution list to friends and co-workers highlighting local events and happenings. The list grew exponentially as those included on the first lists forwarded Craigslist to friends who then forwarded it to their friends. Because Craigslist never bothered to define itself, it soon became a website for nearly anything and everything you needed. People used it as an online garage sale. People used it to search for certain things they wanted to buy. People even used it to innocuously advertise themselves, a precursor to the online dating services that now abound.

From the moment Craigslist was born, it started expanding, and fifteen years after Newmark founded it, it hasn't stopped yet. In less than a year the website moved into other cities. After incorporation as a private for-profit company in 1999, Craigslist expanded into nine more U.S. cities in 2000, four each in 2001 and 2002 and fourteen in 2003.

By the time of the murder of Julissa Brisman, Craigslist had established itself in approximately 700 cities in seventy countries. Today it operates with a staff of only twenty-eight people. Craigslist charges only for job advertisements and real estate sales postings. They get $75 per job ad in San Franciso and $25 per ad in New York, Boston, Chicago, San Diego, Seattle, Philadelphia, Washington D.C., and Portland, Oregon. Real estate brokers have to cough up a pittance for apartment listings in cities like New York by paying $10 per ad. All the other postings are free.

Craigslist claims to have over twenty billion page views per month, putting it in thirtieth place overall among websites worldwide and eighth place in web hits in the United States, where some 50 million people per month browse the site. With over eighty million new classified advertisements each month, Craigslist is the leading classifieds service in any medium and receives over one million new employment listings a month, making it one of the leading job boards in the world. In fact, because of the huge volume in free or cheap classified and job listings, Craigslist has often been blamed for almost single-handedly causing the demise of the American newspaper industry.

Newmark has told reporters that Craigslist works because it gives people a voice, a sense of community trust and even intimacy. Other factors he cites are consistency of down-to-earth values, customer service and simplicity.

Another reason for Craigslist's popularity and

growth, though one Newmark would never acknowledge publicly, is the free and usually raunchy sex ads.

Like the other products advertised on Craigslist there is no end to the variety of human flesh being offered and the type of sexual acts they're willing to perform. There are casual encounters and bondage hookups and prostitutes and happy endings. Whatever fetish you're into, you can find it on Craigslist: women for men, men for men, women for women, transvestites, transgender, transsexual, etc.

Newmark claims that Craigslist uses a user flagging system to quickly identify illegal and inappropriate postings. Congress and law enforcement officials say the flagging system does not go nearly far enough. Shortly after Markoff was arrested, given the spate of Craigslist-related killings, politicians were making noise about holding hearings to see if Craigslist and other social networking websites should be held more accountable for the activities being advertised on them.

The day after Rhode Island attorney general Patrick Lynch held his press conference announcing Markoff's arrest warrant, another lawmaker urged Craigslist to be a responsible corporate entity. In South Carolina, Attorney General Henry McMaster wrote a letter to Craigslist's CEO, a businessman named Jim Buckmaster.

"Many of the classified and communication services on the Craigslist site provide the public with a valuable service," the attorney general wrote on May

5, 2009. "However, it appears that the management of Craigslist has knowingly allowed the site to be used for illegal and unlawful activity after warnings from law enforcement officials and after an agreement with 40 state attorneys general."

Those attorneys general felt like Craigslist had failed to live up to a promise the company had made to law enforcement officials from across the country to improve the site's safeguards and eliminate illegal activities, specifically prostitution.

But Craigslist wasn't moving fast enough for South Carolina. McMaster was threatening to prosecute the company if it didn't step up and "remove the portions of the Internet site dedicated to South Carolina and its municipal regions which contain categories for and functions allowing for the solicitation of prostitution and the dissemination and posting of graphic pornographic material" within ten days.

The company CEO was forced to issue a press release:

"We anticipate making further progress toward the common goal of eliminating illegal activity from Craigslist while preserving its full utility and benefit for tens of millions of law-abiding Americans who value and depend on Craigslist's free local community services in their everyday use," Buckmaster wrote.

But he also sued the South Carolina AG seeking an injunction preventing McMaster to file the charges he had been threatening the company with.

But some law enforcement officials were sick of words from the company. They wanted concrete action. The turned to the congressional delegation for help and began to tick off the other Craigslist-connected homicides that had been marked in the United States.

Weeks before Julissa Brisman was brutally murdered, a radio reporter from Brooklyn, New York, who posted a Craigslist ad looking for rough gay sex had been slain.

The victim's name was George Weber. He had offered $60 for an anonymous encounter with a "top," or a man who took charge in an S&M encounter. He had no idea that the troubled teen who answered his ad was a Satan-loving sadomasochist and hustler. The teen, John Katehis, later told police that he had a knife fetish. He admitted to stabbing Weber "fifty times" to the neck and body, NYPD officials would announce. Despite his spontaneous confession, he has pleaded not guilty.

"He and Weber met online sometime last week and had arranged to meet," Police Commissioner Raymond Kelly told reporters in a press conference at One Police Plaza on March 24, 2009. "There was going to be an exchange of money."

After the murder which happened on a Friday, Katehis shed his bloody clothes and fled wearing some of Weber's clothes. He ended up in custody after a subway train conductor spotted his bleeding left hand and called police, Kelly said.

Katehis told cops at Elmhurst Hospital Center in Queens, New York, that he cut his hand on a bottle, Kelly said. Weber's body wasn't found until Sunday, so cops had no idea Katehis might be a killer. They let him go and he fled upstate to Middletown in Orange County, New York, hoping to hide out at a friend's house. When cops finally nabbed him, Katehis was still dressed in Weber's clothes, Kelly said.

Katehis admitted stabbing Weber, a longtime WABC reporter, after answering an ad on Craigslist. If Weber had Googled the teen who answered his ad he may have stumbled upon his MySpace account. Had he seen it, Weber might have had second thoughts about letting Katehis in his home. Katehis posted pictures of himself with various knives—including one he held against his neck. He also issued a chilling warning. "If you disrespect me then I will f——g break your neck," he wrote, according to the New York *Daily News*. On his site, Katehis called himself "Extremist, an Anarchist, a Sadomasochist" and said he enjoyed "long conversations, drinking, bike riding, hanging out." The teen also listed more reckless hobbies such as "roof hopping, hanging off trains" and violent video games, the *News* reported.

"I am a very easy person to talk to," he wrote. "I'm always looking for a big thrill." Katehis's lawyer, Herb Moses, blamed the victim.

"It's a very tragic situation. I think he was used by an older gentleman," Moses said.

Weber, forty-seven, had been recently laid off from

WABC where he had worked as an on-air reporter for a decade. He freelanced for ABC's national radio network and wrote a blog. A private memorial service was held at Weber's home after relatives and friends toasted his memory with shots of Wild Turkey at the newsman's favorite bar, Angry Wade's. "I really wish people knew George the way we knew George," close pal John Peterman, thirty-five, told the *News* reporter.

Weber's friends were media types. They believed in the First Amendment. But when there was talk of asking Craigslist to step up its safety standards, the people who loved George Weber agreed.

And his case was not the only one. The first Craigslist-associated murder happened in Cottage Grove, Minnesota, in October 2007. A twenty-four-year-old woman named Katherine Ann Olson answered a Craigslist ad for a nanny and was later found murdered.

Katherine Ann had grown up in a very religious family—her father was a pastor—and was extremely trusting of strangers. That trusting nature got her shot and killed. Her bloody body was found in the trunk of her car in a public park in Minnesota. She had told her family where she was going and police searched her computer and found the nanny advertisement, which they traced to a nineteen-year-old named Michael John Anderson, an airport employee with a history of mental illness. At the time of his arrest, the media in Minnesota dubbed Anderson the "Craigslist killer." Anderson was sentenced to life in prison on April 2, 2009—eighteen days before Philip Markoff was arrested as another suspected "Craigslist Killer."

Prosecutors said during the weeklong trial that Anderson, of Savage, Minnesota, ran a phony ad on Craigslist in order to lure a woman to his home so he might experience what it felt like to kill.

"Why did you do this? You are the only one who knows and I won't pretend to understand it," Scott County district judge Mary Theisen said from the bench. She added that Anderson was a "coward" when he shot Olson—who Theisen believed was "running for her life."

Sarah Richter, Olson's older sister, said her sleep is interrupted nightly by horrible images caused by the first Craigslist Killer. "I'm haunted by Anderson's face, by Katherine's screams, the gun, her body in the trunk and now, the real bloody images of my sister. When will I sleep again?"

Craigslist founder Craig Newmark was so moved by the woman's murder, he made a personal contribution to the Katherine Ann Olson fund at a concert organized in Eden Prairie, Minnesota, in her honor. He wrote that check for an undisclosed amount two weeks after Philip Markoff was arrested.

By then Craigslist was getting more than a little bad ink and the skeptical saw Newmark's donation as an attempt at damage control.

"I'm saddened that we met in these circumstances,

but I am truly inspired by the Olson family," Newmark said. He also added that her murder, along with the slaying of Julissa Brisman, were reminders that "truly evil intentions do exist."

"Despite the billions of times well-meaning people have helped each other through Craigslist, it's been devastating to see that it can also be used by bad people to take cruel advantage of others." Newmark made these remarks from the stage of the fundraising concert. Flanked by Olson's family, he repeated himself, "Truly evil."

He was so right. Less than two months after Julissa was murdered, another Craigslist killing would be splashed across the headlines. This time it took place in Oregon. The victim was pregnant and hoping to get some cheap baby clothes by answering an ad on Craigslist. Instead she met her killer.

Heather Snively, twenty-one, was found dead in the crawlspace of a rented home in a gritty neighborhood in Tigard, Oregon. She was in her third trimester. Her stomach had been slashed open, her baby removed. Police arrested a troubled twenty-seven-year-old woman who apparently used to the ad to lure a pregnant woman to her home so she could kill her and take the baby, who also died, to raise as her own.

On the victim's Facebook page a family member posted: "Something truly awful has happened in my family. Please pray for us because we are going to need it."

By then the pressure on Craigslist was unrelenting. So the company took what appeared to be action.

Craigslist scrapped its "erotic services" ads. They replaced it with an "adult" section which the company says is more carefully monitored.

Law enforcement officials think Craigslist was just trying to pull a fast one. "Rather than work with this office to prevent further abuses, in the middle of the night Craigslist took unilateral action which we suspect will prove to be half-baked," said New York attorney general Andrew Cuomo.

Connecticut attorney general Richard Blumenthal announced that he was "encouraged" but said that he wanted to make sure that the "online red light district" was going to invoke real change, not just "a name change."

Patrick Lynch in Rhode Island wanted the change in some sort of formal piece of legislation, given that the company had made a similar agreement in the past but had reneged. Massachusetts attorney general Martha Coakley was about to embark on a political campaign for United States Senate for the seat made vacant by Ted Kennedy's death. She was too busy campaigning to make a real push to censor Craigslist.

In an interview with ABC News, Newmark defended the company, pointing out that Craigslist had helped law enforcement in the past.

"My first reaction is sympathy; I mean I feel pretty bad for the victims and their families. I don't like it at all. Beyond that, well, how would you feel if . . . the bad guy watched what you do on TV and started calling [you] the 'ABC Killer'? That's pretty much how I'm reacting," Newmark said. "It just feels bad. You know, remember, I'm spending a great deal of time here fighting bad guys."

Many crime fighters disagreed.

"Craigslist is the largest source of prostitution in America," said Cook County, Illinois, sheriff Tom Dart, who eventually filed a federal lawsuit trying to ban Craigslist from continuing to offer its "erotic services" section because it promoted prostitution.

Newmark, however, defended his baby on *ABC News*, saying that his site does not facilitate prostitution.

"Sometimes a bad guy of some sort tries to pull a fast one on our site. We don't want it there, it's wrong, and that's why we have the help of the general community and the law enforcement community getting rid of things like that," he said.

Newmark had a point. Even if one were to suspect someone was engaged in prostitution, the folks at Craigslist were not vice detectives. And as far as the Craigslist-related murders, how could the politicians blame Craigslist for the actions of demented, psychotic killers?

Newmark pointed out that with 50 million users per month in the United States alone, "I'm very proud that our site is composed of people who are overwhelmingly trustworthy and good. I am very proud that there is very little crime on our site, proportionately. Compare that to any other American community, look at the numbers."

As a private company, Craigslist is under no obligation to publish its financial records, and it never has. But industry experts estimate the site made between $60 and $80 million last year alone. Newmark offered to donate 100 percent of its "adult services" revenues to charities, such as those trying to eradicate missing or exploited children.

It was not enough to appease Congress. In June of 2009, twenty-six Congressmen wrote to Newmark saying they were "disturbed by the number of violent crimes that have resulted from the 'Erotic Services' section of Craigslist" and called on Craigslist to reform the website's practices. The Congressmen also asked for a written response and a formal meeting with Craigslist big shots.

"The evidence suggests that Craigslist's 'Erotic Services' section abetted unlawful commercial sex trafficking," the letter read. "It seems clear that anyone viewing the listings would recognize the purpose and illegality of them."

The letter cited the fact that in addition to the murders, at least fifty women have been raped or severely beaten in the last two years by men who responded to ads on Craigslist. That number, of course, only includes those women who report a crime. The real number is anyone's guess. The members of Congress specifically took issue with Craigslist's attempt to rectify the complaints from McMaster and other attorneys general by moving the "erotic services" to a new "adult services" section the previous month.

"We have a series of questions that we hope will demonstrate your commitment to ending the violence which has resulted from [this section]," they wrote. "It is imperative that creating an 'Adult Services' section to replace the aforementioned section must not simply shift the same solicitations to a newly entitled section, but instead must lead to fundamental change."

But very little has changed at the company. Changing the section name from "erotic" to "adult" services was just that and nothing more. There are still plenty of transvestites available for one-night stands, professionals offering "sensual hand massage" for $200 and strippers offering up private lap dances.

Click on Craigslist today, go under "Boston," click on "Adult$" under the "services" section, and you'll still find ads like the one posted December 20, 2009, which sported a headline, "Gorgeous**Hot** Blonde**" followed by "W4M," women for men. There's a picture of a busty, blonde-haired woman wearing a white bikini bathing suit. The picture is cropped to show just the lower half of her face." Hi guys my name is Sharon I am a fun loving blonde thats [sic] ready for some fun. If your [sic] ready for something new so am I**."

"This is Sharon," a gravely-voiced woman answers a call placed to the cell phone number.

The caller asked if she was available later that

night and she said she was. Where are you located? "The Westin," she said. Not the one at Copley Place where Trisha Leffler was tied up and robbed by the Craigslist Killer but another Westin in the Boston suburb of Waltham.

How much?

"It's a hundred dollars an hour, honey," she said.

18

It's amazing how the mind works.

When Philip Markoff first arrived at Suffolk County Jail all he could think about was killing himself; ending the humiliation, the never-ending stories about his dark side, squelching the fear of prison. Two times in the first ten days he tried suicide, twice it failed.

Less than two months later, Philip Markoff had surprisingly settled into the prison life. He was no longer on suicide watch and had been allowed to wear a prison uniform instead of a paper hospital gown or padded anti-suicide smock. He was also moved into the main part of the jail known by prisoners as "general population." He seemingly got along well with most of the other inmates—especially Jeffrey McGee, the man who stood accused of killing his wife because he suspected she was sleeping with the lead singer of the heavy metal band Godsmack.

Markoff had a few visitors now and then. His mother came around once a month. His father stopped by. His stepfather, Gary Carroll, came twice. So did an uncle from upstate New York, Gary's brother Greg Carroll. There was a friend named Steven Lee from Somerville, Massachusetts, who refused to talk to reporters about the nature of his relationship with Markoff. And a woman who knew Markoff as a kid, Patricia Parrotte, who lived in Utica, New York, came once. No one was talking. Letters sent to their homes by a reporter went unanswered. Richard Markoff went as far as to demand that the letter be returned to sender unopened.

Markoff had become, if not comfortable, at least accustomed to prison life. He settled into a routine which included some of his old habits. To pass the hours, he set up poker games and played blackjack with his fellow cons. Of course, he was always the dealer when it came to blackjack. He knew the odds by then: The house always won, especially against novices. In fact, in his high school yearbook back in Sherrill, he had bequeathed his "poker playing skills" to a classmate. He wasn't kidding. "The kid is a card shark," one deputy sheriff, who was charged with supervising Markoff, would remark. "It earned him some friends, some respect. He gets along."

Meanwhile, Megan McAllister was counting the days until she could leave for St. Kitts—hoping there's no way the Craigslist Killer story had enough "legs," as they said in the news business, to swim all

the way to the Caribbean. Until then, she was cooperating with investigators, having already testified in
front of the grand jury. Grand jury testimony is supposed to remain secret by law and law enforcement
officials are notoriously guarded about revealing
anything that was talked about behind those closed
doors in the Suffolk County Superior Courthouse.
But two sources familiar with what McAllister said
were willing to share some of what the devastated
young woman told the grand jury.

McAllister said she was out of town planning their
wedding when her fiancé allegedly struck. She was
in New Jersey listening to CDs of potential wedding
bands when Philip Markoff drove to a gun store in
Mason, New Hampshire, and flashed a New York
driver's license with the name Andrew Miller—a
college buddy of his—to purchase the 9mm at the
State Line Gun Shop.

With a state motto of "Live Free or Die," New
Hampshire is certainly a gun-friendly state. Still,
there are a few laws in place for gun purchases there;
you have to have some sort of authentic identification proving you are who you are claiming to be
and you have to prove you're a New Hampshire resi-
dent. Then:

"They would go to the licensed gun dealer, someone that holds a federal firearms license, and that
person would provide the dealer with some form of
ID," said Sgt. Chris Scott of New Hampshire State
Police. "The dealer would then take that information

and provide that to the New Hampshire State Police Instant Gun Line.

"The person working the state police gun line runs a background check through criminal databases, which only takes a couple of minutes. The store is then told to approve, deny or delay the sale. Something like a felony conviction or domestic-violence-related arrest may mean the person is denied. A delay gives the state three days to verify whether any questions on a person's background should prevent them from buying the gun."

Of course, Markoff had no criminal history that would have prohibited him from buying a gun. And apparently there were also no red flags in the background of Andrew Miller, the man whose New York driver's license Markoff handed to the gun dealer. It was not a dupe, it was Miller's actual license, which a Suffolk County District Attorney's Office spokesman said "hadn't been doctored in any way." The spokesman, however, did admit that the appearances of the two men were "somewhat similar."

Never missing an opportunity to get his name in the papers, when Boston's district attorney, Daniel Conley, discovered how the gun that was used to kill Julissa Brisman was purchased, he made a big stink about how New Hampshire should toughen its gun laws.

The owner of the State Line Gun Shop, Paul Gauffin, declined interviews with all the large media outlets. But he did speak to his tiny little twice-weekly community newspaper and claimed that he followed all the proper procedures. And he said Conley was wrong in assuming that they didn't do their due diligence before selling Markoff his gun.

"He came in with a New York driver's license and proof of residency in New Hampshire," Gauffin told the *Monadanock Ledger-Tribune*. "We faxed the documents off to New Hampshire State Police, they approved the sale and that's all there was to it."

Gauffin said New Hampshire's gun laws require that the identification used only be authentic, not issued from New Hampshire. And he added that there was a very strong resemblance between the man he sold the gun to and the picture on the ID he provided.

"Obviously, this is the first time we've ever had anything like this happen," Gauffin said. "We follow the law completely and don't feel liability toward the death of this poor woman (Brisman). Mr. Markoff committed three or four felonies in the purchase of the firearm, never mind whatever else. Criminals will find a way; they are not concerned about breaking the law."

In fact, the local district attorney in Gauffin's county said no criminal charges would be filed in the case.

No matter who was to blame for the gun sale, the purchase did provide police with more evidence against Markoff. They lifted Markoff's prints off the purchasing documents he filled out at the State

Line Gun Shop. Just another brick in the case that prosecution was building against Markoff.

As was Megan McAllister's grand jury testimony. McAllister told the grand jurists she was in New Jersey planning her wedding during the week of her then-fiancé's alleged crime spree. "I had no idea what he was doing," she told one detective. "I talked to him on the phone every day, and nothing seemed weird."

According to that same detective, Megan was not by any stretch of the imagination an "idiot." She was just a girl who was in love. She was treated like a princess. Philip doted on her, brought her breakfast in bed, fresh flowers, anything she wanted.

"She definitely did not want to believe he was capable of the things he was accused of," the detective said.

Megan became more cooperative when she learned that the panties and the gun were hidden under *their* bed, the detective said. That's how she said it. *THEIR* bed as if it was in bold type, italicized and underlined. It was an affront to everything she believed about him. Her lawyer put it in writing. She was in New Jersey from March 20 through April 18, and returned to the Quincy apartment just as cops had begun their surveillance of 8 Highpoint Circle.

On June 11, after testifying in front of the grand jury, McAllister visited the Nashua Street jail—for the last time. She was very clear about that point. A source said she told Markoff, "This is the last time

I'm coming here." She meant it. But saying it out loud made her eyes well up with tears nevertheless.

McAllister didn't hide that visit to her former fiancé, though. It was just the opposite, in fact. She wanted everyone to know why she came to see the supposed Craigslist Killer again and what she was there to tell him. Her lawyer, Robert Honecker, made a statement to reporters after she left the jail that day. "She told him that she planned to attend medical school and also she let him know that she did not expect to return to Boston and it would be quite a long period of time, if ever, before she saw him again." Honecker then confirmed that McAllister was cooperating with the grand jury.

"Megan will always love and support the man she knew," Honecker said. "She will await the legal process and she will hopefully abide by what is the determination of time and the court of law as to what is the real Philip Markoff."

The *real Philip Markoff*. Could Markoff even be sure who that was anymore? Had he ever known? Suddenly he wanted to die again.

When Megan left, Markoff was visibly upset. He was "picking at his skin so hard he drew blood," a deputy sheriff, who spoke on the condition of anonymity, would say. "It was then that he began to start hoarding medication." Inmates in Massachusetts prisons have access to unbelievably good health care. Markoff's first failed suicide attempt meant he had a full-time shrink. That shrink gave him anti-anxiety medications. He stopped taking them as prescribed and instead stockpiled them. The piles of pills, anti-anxiety medication, would send Markoff for yet another stint in the suicide unit days later. It would be short-lived. By the time of his next court appearance, the day that he would be formally indicted on murder charges, Markoff was shaven and back in the general population area of the Nashua Street jail, playing cards with the guys.

Amazing how the mind works.

This time he would not only have to avoid the stares of his own family, he would have to make sure he didn't lock eyes with Carmen Guzman, the grieving mother of Julissa Brisman. She was in the courtroom with her daughter and a translator. It would not be easy for her to hear the case against her daughter's accused killer, but she was ready to finally see him; the man who stood accused of taking away her baby, snuffing out Julissa's young life just as it started to move along the right track.

It was June 22, 2009. Markoff had been behind bars for two months and two days. His legal worries were continuing to escalate.

By then, Suffolk County district attorney Ed Zabin had taken the lead on the investigation. He was small but ruggedly built, a bulldog in the homicide unit of the understaffed and overburdened district attorney's office.

Zabin began his career as a Suffolk County prosecutor in 1993. Steadily Zabin was promoted up the district attorney's office ladder, becoming supervisor of one of their criminal court offices in 1995 where misdemeanors were tried, then getting promoted to Superior Court to try the heavy cases. In 2002, Conley promoted Zabin to the Homicide Unit.

Immediately, Zabin was handling the high-profile cases and almost always winning. He obtained a first-degree murder conviction on a man who stabbed Suffolk County sheriff's deputy Richard Dever, who was trying to break up a bar fight in March 2005. Zabin also put Euclides Oritz behind bars for life for stabbing his wife, Bernice, in 2003, trying to get her out of the picture because Ortiz had impregnated his girlfriend. Zabin obtained another life sentence in the case of a Moroccan immigrant teen who was killed outside a movie theater by a man who had tried, unsuccessfully, to rob him earlier in the week. "Remember me?" Darryl Scott said before shooting eighteen-year-old Nabil Essaid outside a downtown Boston movie theater.

In 2005, Zabin was named a "Super Lawyer" by *Boston* magazine and received the Suffolk Award for Outstanding Superior Court Prosecutor the same year. There were a lot of "Super Lawyers" in the Craigslist Killer case. They were drawn to TV cameras like flies swarmed around shit.

In 2006, Conley tapped Zabin to serve in the dual capacity of deputy chief of the Homicide Unit and chief of the Senior Trial Unit—a team of prosecutors, Conley said, "who handle some of the most serious and complex violent crimes committed in Suffolk County." In January 2008, Conley made Zabin his homicide chief. In that job, Zabin was overseeing the homicide investigations in more than 40 percent of the homicides that take place in the entire state of Massachusetts each year. As such, Zabin couldn't try as many cases as he did in the past. Only the big ones. The Craigslist Killer was a big one.

As the charges against his son were read, Richard Markoff unconsciously rocked back and forth in his seat. Susan Haynes twitched her hands nervously in her lap. Markoff's brother, Jonathan, was also in court alongside his wife, Deanna, whom he held hands with throughout the arraignment. Asked if he still believed in his son's innocence, Richard Markoff nodded yes. What else could he do?

The indictment was detailed. In February of 2009, Markoff purchased several disposable TracFone cell phones. Again, another hint for prosecutors that Markoff may have victimized people long before April when Trisha Leffler was attacked in Boston, Julissa Brisman was murdered when she put up a fight in a neighboring hotel two months later and when Cynthia Melton was assaulted in Rhode Island. Markoff, according to the indictment, used those phones to contact all three of those victims.

The stupidest move he made was keeping those TracFones. They were found in his apartment. He even kept the receipts, making investigators' jobs even easier. The indictment also described the gun in the hollowed-out copy of *Gray's Anatomy*. It was a 9mm Springfield Armory XD-9 semiautomatic. The indictment also said that they could link four pairs of panties rolled up into a pair of socks to the victims Trisha Leffler and Cynthia Melton. Brisman's murder happened too fast for him to snatch a pair.

The indictment also talked about a black Toshiba laptop that Markoff used not only for his medical homework but to email his victims. There were "remnants," prosecutors said, of the emails that Markoff had sent to Julissa Brisman on the night she died.

All of those details would play out in court.

At 11:01 a.m. Philip Markoff entered the courtroom. His ankles were shackled with leg irons. The court was packed but the sounds of the iron chains were audible as they dragged across the floor as he approached the defendant's bench. This time his hair was neatly cut by the prison barber. His white shirt was not rumpled. Again, he did not once look toward his family in the back rows. And he certainly didn't look at Julissa's family.

Brisman's mother Carmen Guzman cried as Markoff made his pleas, "Not guilty." Brisman's sister bowed her head and began to cry audibly when prosecutors reread the details of the attack, during which they said Brisman was "hit on the head before being shot at point blank range three times."

Zabin also talked about the Bureau of Alcohol, Tobacco and Firearms and how agents traced the murder weapon to the New Hampshire shop and found Markoff's prints on the purchasing document, prosecutors said. Those prints also matched those found at the scene of Brisman's killing, the D.A. said in court.

Andrew Miller is cooperating with the investigation, said Zabin, who did not comment on how Markoff and Miller knew each other. Brisman was found by authorities with one flex-cuff restraint on her wrist and bruising on her other wrist. Zabin said that surveillance video of Markoff shows that he wore the same outfit—a baseball cap and a button-down shirt—on April 10, when he allegedly tied up and robbed a prostitute named Trisha Leffler in the Westin Copley Place hotel, and on April 14, the night Julissa was murdered.

Salsberg may be good, but he was now forced to grasp at straws. He presented the district attorney's office a list of questions he had about media leaks, information that has been used in this book. Salsberg said that he will argue that "the jury pool has been poisoned." In fact, in the months after he took on the Craigslist Killer case and Markoff as his client, it had become his mantra. *The jury pool had been poisoned, the jury pool has been poisoned*, as if there's a jury in another part of Massachusetts that might be willing to overlook the mountain of evidence compiled against Markoff: the duct tape, the zip-ties, the gun, the fingerprints, the emails, the Trac-Fone calls, the surveillance photos, the witness identification. And the testimony of the one woman who stuck by him, the woman who had previously insisted that her fiancé would "not hurt a fly" but now obviously wasn't so sure anymore.

Carmen Guzman was too distraught to talk to reporters. She instead released a statement which was read to the assembled press.

"I feel very much relieved that the man who did this is in custody and will not be able to do this horrible thing to another family. Our family has been devastated by the loss of our beautiful daughter Julissa. We are a close family and Julissa called us every day. We won't be getting those calls anymore. Over the past few days people have told us the many ways in which Julissa helped them. Her friends say Julissa was like a bright light, full of energy and optimism, always ready to help other people. These words mean so much to us.

"The feeling of losing my daughter in this way, and the pain she must have felt, will haunt me for the rest of my life. She won't live to see her dreams. We will hold Julissa in our hearts every day."

Suffolk County district attorney Dan Conley had a message of his own for the people who loved Julissa. Conley put a reassuring hand on Guzman's shoulder and said in Spanish:

"We will do everything we can for you."

It would be enough for Carmen Guzman and her family if Philip Markoff—not the Craigslist Killer, but Philip Markoff the man who police believe killed their beautiful Julissa—would spend the rest of his life rotting in jail. And that's exactly what was likely to happen.

19

In the winter of 2009—as the Craigslist Killer settled into life in prison—Julissa Brisman became a central figure in the hopes and aspirations of another infamous case involving the online sex trade.

Eliot Spitzer, the sex-crazed former governor and attorney general from New York, seemingly flushed his once-limitless political career down the toilet to have a $2,000-an-hour encounter with a wannabe pop star from the Jersey Shore turned escort who called herself Ashley Dupré. But a little over a year after Spitzer exited public life a completely disgraced man, he slowly started making the rounds again.

In March 2009, Spitzer did an interview on CNN in which he admitted, "I failed in a very important way in my personal life, and I have paid a price for that. . . . I have spent a year with my family—with my wonderful and amazing and forgiving wife and three daughters—and we'll rebuild those relationships, and hope to do that as time goes on," he said.

When asked about his future plans, Spitzer said, "I also feel [that] if I'm asked, and I can contribute to a very important conversation, I will do that as well. I will do what I can—and with full awareness and heaviness of heart about what I did."

As the decade came to an end and 2010 got underway, some in the Spitzer camp were floating trial balloons for his re-entrance into public life. A planned run was hinted at, this time as New York's comptroller.

At least one opponent sprang up immediately. Kirstin Davis, the "Manhattan Madam," announced that she too will enter the Democratic primary for New York state comptroller, if Spitzer joins the race. And she predicted that she'd win.

On her website, www.manhattanmadam.com, Davis gave her reasons for wanting to mount a run against Spitzer. At the very least she was going to demand that the man who sent her to prison have the guts to show up at some debates and face her bulging bosom and Botox-enhanced looks and those lips plumped with filler.

She wrote: "Client Number 9 is talking to potential fundraisers and political consultants about a comeback bid. If Eliot Spitzer runs I will take the plunge and enter the Democratic primary for New York State Comptroller.

"If I run, I will advocate the legalization, regulation and taxation of both prostitution and marijuana to solve New York's fiscal problems. Eliot Spitzer,

Andrew Cuomo, and Tom DiNapoli offer only tax increases, more borrowing, greater debt and service cuts: I will offer a plan for new revenues from two activities that are going to happen anyway. Under my plan New York's budget can be balanced without raising taxes on working people or cuts to vital services. Who else can say that? Prostitution should be legalized for both the public safety and to fill the public coffers. No more Craig's List [*sic*] murders. No more Johns robbed. Regular medical checkups and licensing of service providers by the State."

She said her political motivation came about after the death of Julissa.

In interviews Davis said that she was running to honor the memory of her slain friend Julissa Brisman. "I was shocked, devastated, heartbroken, but I wasn't surprised," says Davis. "I told her to be careful. Craigslist is full of creeps." That was for sure. The bad publicity for Craigslist in 2009 continued to mount. There were more arrests, more Craigslist killers. Like twenty-four-year-old Shawn Skelton in Kent, Washington, who was busted after he allegedly posted a Craigslist ad titled "A strange desire," looking for a woman to have sex with and then kill.

The ad read: "Young dude looking for a good time. We'll get drinks, go back to my place, and then I'll kill you!"

An undercover vice detective, flagged by a Craigslist employee (something that its executives would crow about to investigators calling for their heads), responded to Shawn's ad. The two exchanged about thirty e-mails over the next several days in which Shawn described what sex acts he was going to perform on her before he killed her, and he may have alluded to the manner in which she would die. The two agreed to meet at a Seattle motel. At the last second, Shawn doubled the asking price to $2,000. The meeting was set for Monday morning. When Shawn knocked on the motel door, he was taken down and arrested. A search revealed that Shawn had come prepared. He was packing a knife, a heavy chain, and two long shoestrings. Shawn later confessed to the attempted murder and said he needed help. According to investigators, the suspect told them "this activity excited him and admitted that he needed counseling and could not control his urges." Shawn is now controlling his urges behind bars held on a $1 million bond. And then in early May convicted sex offender John Steven Burgess pleaded guilty in Los Angeles to involuntary manslaughter in the death of nineteen-year-old Donna Jou. Burgess said he plied Jou with alcohol, cocaine and heroin after meeting her on Craigslist, then dumped her body in the ocean when she overdosed.

Sure, taking on Craigslist was a good platform if one was a prostitute and madam who wanted to try her hands in a very similar business to selling oneself—politics. Cynics thought the Manhattan Madam's motive was rooted in an old adage: Hell hath no fury like a woman scorned. She almost backed up that belief with her own words. Eliot Spitzer, whom she derides as the "Steamroller," sent her to jail for months. He wrecked her business. Craigslist didn't help either. Why pay a madam when you can find a hooker for free?

"Many of my friends asked me why I became so 'political.' Sitting on Rikers for four months gives you plenty of time to think. I thought about the unfairness of our system and the total incompetence of our elected officials who can't get a gay marriage bill passed. Then Philip Markoff [allegedly] murdered my friend and former employee Julissa Brisman and I decided to start speaking out. I spent months wondering if one person speaking out can make a difference. I think it can."

She continued:

"Eliot Spitzer violated the public trust. His hypocrisy, patronizing escort services while prosecuting others . . ."

To make matters worse, as the entire country learned, Spitzer refused to take off his black dress socks while sleeping with Davis's call girls. Plus, he was rough with them.

"His black socks in the boudoir are an additional affront to good taste. His abuse of some of the woman that I arranged for him to spend time with raises serious questions about his character."

The madam-turned-political candidate finished;

"I am ready to match my ideas with the Steamroller—not to mention asking him some pointed questions. I am ready to throw my hat in the ring. I will be the first candidate in New York history to run while on probation. See you at the debates, Eliot."

Kristin Davis announced her intention to run against Spitzer in December of 2009. Philip Markoff—the man who murdered her "friend and former employee"—was getting into some trouble of his own that month.

Once again he engaged in some prison shenanigans that would land him back in the segregation unit. It would also lead him to declare to prison officials:

"They got me. I'm going away forever. What's a little hooch?"

20

Just because the investigation into Philip Markoff's crime spree was on solid footing didn't mean the Boston Police homicide division had stopped working in the time since he was arrested.

In fact it was quite the opposite. They continued to pull together the threads of the lives of this Dr. Jekyll and Mr. Hyde character, or rather the once future Dr. Markoff and his devilish counterpart, the Craigslist Killer.

Cops had listed 177 pieces of evidence against Markoff. Searches were conducted at Markoff's apartment in Quincy, his book locker at Boston University, and the cars he drove, including a Toyota Corolla registered to his former fiancée, Megan McAllister, and a Chevrolet Trailblazer registered to his mother. Every single piece of evidence collected against Markoff had been logged by cops. Salsberg wanted to know exactly what he was up against. He was entitled to know, in fact. So he demanded a list of discovery materials. He certainly got one. There were some surprising items listed and some not so surprising.

It seemed that Conley may have found a link to another victim in New Bedford, according to the discovery list. That phone call from a woman in New Bedford, a notorious hotbed of prostitution, could mean another victim had encountered Phil Markoff. Dan Conley—through his spokesman Jake Wark—had no comment. "We cannot confirm or deny," said Wark, who was familiar with that statement. His job depended on it.

The list provided a road map of the entire case from the time the first woman was attacked in the Boston hotel room on April 10 and including every single move made by Boston police investigators during the Craigslist Killer's crime spree. The document contained every piece of evidence that had been gathered against Philip Markoff in the time since his arrest. Forensic evidence that had been gathered against him. Search warrants. Fingerprints. Interviews. Phone calls. Phone records. A list of interviews conducted. The trips to Foxwoods. The emails sent to transvestites. Pages of documentation relating to the murder of Julissa Brisman. Police reports that detailed the attack on Trisha Leffler. Interview transcripts from the time cops spent with Cynthia Melton.

There was a sixty-two-page interview with Philip Markoff. A damning interview for Markoff and one that made Jon Salsberg's job a lot more difficult. Hard to defend a guy who spilled his guts, and the transcript of the interview was an indication that he had spilled his guts. That's a lot of talking, sixty-two pages.

The list also showed Megan was absolutely cooperating with investigators who planned to put away her former fiancé for life. She had talked to detectives. The transcript of that conversation numbered seventy-eight pages. Staggering. She would be forced to testify against her fiancé. She had already testified in front of the grand jury. She made herself available for follow-up questions. His locker, his house, his cars had been searched. Foxwoods had handed over its records. Verizon handed over bills. Cable provided Internet access records. Police believed Markoff apparently dropped off his blood-splattered clothes to Dependable Cleaners after Brisman's murder. Prosecutors even obtained an application Markoff made to the United States Bowling Commissioner for a special award. It seemed that the great Boston homicide squad investigators managed to convince Cynthia Melton and her husband Keith Melton—the Rhode Island victims—to cooperate. They too picked Phil Markoff out of a photo lineup. Julissa Brisman's four-page rap sheet was part of the case, because cops could be sure that John Salsberg would bring it up. The evidence against Phil Markoff was extraordinary.

There were also 101 pages of grand jury minutes, testimony from an array of people who knew or had had dealings with Philip Markoff. Megan McAllister's testimony was among those grand jury pages and her two interviews with police detectives among the pile of documents that would eventually shape the prosecution's case against her former lover.

Among the stranger items listed as evidence was a U.S. Bowling Congress Special Achievement award given to a Philip H. Markoff, who was listed as a member of its Albany association. Another item was a reservation Markoff made with U-Haul. The prosecution's notice of discovery indicates police searched Markoff's locker No. 15 at Boston University Medical School. There were printouts from Craigslist, including the posting "Hot Brunette Model & Massuse [sic] - visting Today." That was the one that Mary Beth Simons sent out to entice new clients for Julissa Brisman or "Morgan," as she called herself. At that point, of course, Simons had no idea that she was providing the cyber connection that would lead to her close friend's murder.

Boston district attorney Dan Conley was still milking whatever publicity he could from the successful apprehension of the accused notorious Craiglist Killer and crowed in press releases that the case was moving forward nicely. And so it was.

On June 21, 2009, Conley's office announced that a grand jury had indicted Markoff on seven counts with an extremely detailed press release that did a yeoman's job of summing up the Craigslist Killer case to date.

The indictments charged "PHILIP MARKOFF (D.O.B. 2/12/86) with the April 14 fatal shooting and attempted robbery of 25-year-old Julissa Brisman in the Marriott Copley Place hotel, the April 10 armed robbery of a 29-year-old Las Vegas woman at the Westin Copley Place hotel, the armed and forcible confinement of both women, and two counts of unlawful possession of a firearm. Markoff is not charged with any offenses against any other individuals. Investigators continue to monitor tips phoned in to the Boston Police Homicide Unit and CrimeStoppers Tip Line at 1-800-494-TIPS."

The indictments moved Markoff's case from the Boston Municipal Court to Suffolk Superior Court.

In the course of the two-month grand jury investigation, prosecutors from Conley's Homicide Unit introduced not only the testimony of witnesses, but also dozens of physical exhibits including internet and telephone records obtained through subpoena. The exhibits and testimony suggest that Markoff contacted both victims through advertisements placed on the "Erotic Services" section of the online service Craigslist.

"Contained in those records was a wealth of information, all of it pointing directly at the defendant," Conley said.

Evidence suggests that Markoff scheduled the meeting with his first victim using a disposable TracFone. Shortly after midnight on April 10, prosecutors believe, Markoff met that woman on the Westin hotel's thirteenth floor. Evidence suggests he accompanied her to her room, where he immediately produced a handgun. Wearing gloves, he allegedly ordered her to the ground and bound her wrists behind her back with zip ties—plastic strips used to secure wires and other loose items.

The woman's assailant spent more than fifteen minutes ransacking her hotel room and taking cash and personal items. Before leaving, Markoff allegedly removed his gloves, placed duct tape over her mouth, and cut the phone lines in the room.

Three days later, prosecutors allege, Markoff responded to Brisman's advertisement via email. Using a different Tracfone, he subsequently arranged a meeting for 10 p.m. on April 14 in her room on the twentieth floor of the Marriott. Evidence suggests that the two struggled briefly after he entered, at which time he struck her multiple times in the head with the butt of a 9mm semiautomatic handgun.

"The blows to her head were so sharp and so violent that they fractured her skull," Conley said.

Markoff allegedly proceeded to fire three rounds into Brisman's chest and abdomen from close range, killing her almost instantly. When she was found lying in the threshold of her room a short time later, Brisman had a zip tie on one wrist and bruising on the other. She was rushed to Boston Medical Center, where she was pronounced dead of her injuries.

In the hours and days following Brisman's homicide, Boston police homicide detectives and Suffolk prosecutors obtained the internet protocol address for the email account used to set up the deadly encounter. Using that IP information, homicide investigators learned the physical address from which the email was sent and undertook surveillance of it. On April 19, they observed a man meeting the assailant's description at that address and identified him as Markoff.

Alerted to the investigation and Markoff's status as a student, members of the Boston University Police Department obtained the defendant's college identification photograph for use in an array that was later presented to the surviving victim. That woman identified Markoff as her assailant.

Boston police continued to trail Markoff until they observed him and a female associate leaving his residence with luggage the next day. Believing that he might be preparing to leave the area and having probable cause to search his vehicle, they stopped him as he traveled south on Interstate 95.

Markoff and his associate were transported to Boston Police Headquarters for interviews. Meanwhile, investigators executed a search warrant on his home, recovering a 9mm semiautomatic handgun, ammunition, and zip ties consistent with those used in the attacks. Investigators also recovered four pairs of women's underwear bundled into socks and secreted within his box spring, several TracFones, and laptop computers, including one with remnants of the email communication arranging his meeting with Brisman.

Shortly after 7 p.m., Conley approved a warrant charging him with Brisman's murder. Markoff was held without bail at his arraignment the next morning in Boston Municipal Court.

Conley noted the investigative contributions not only of Boston, State, Transit, and BU police, but also those of Boston police detectives assigned to his Special Investigations Unit; agents of the Federal Bureau of Investigation, the Secret Service, and the Bureau of Alcohol, Tobacco, Firearms, and Explosives; the Cybercrime Division of the Massachusetts Attorney General's office; the Rhode Island Attorney General's office; and the police departments of New York City and Warwick, Rhode Island.

Now it was a waiting game. Conley was ecstatic about putting Phil Markoff away and it seemed as if the trial's verdict was a foregone conclusion. Just another opportunity for the politically ambitious Conley to get more good press, not long before he's up for re-election in November 2010.

By the time August 14, 2009, rolled around, the day that Philip and Megan would have been married, his former fiancée had moved to St. Kitts to attend medical school at the University of Medical and Health Services. Being in the Caribbean was good for her. Reporters had stopped hounding her. Barbara Walters could not reach her there. Neither could Katie Couric or any of the other networks who used the big guns to land an exclusive interview. She wasn't talking, and she was not going to change her mind.

That very day instead of saying "I do," eating some wedding cake, then dancing the night away to the BStreetBand, Philip Markoff was receiving a surprise inspection from deputy sheriff's at his cell inside the Nashua Street jail. What they discovered was a cache of prescribed medication, his anti-anxiety pills, that he had been hoarding away for a second time. Concerned that Philip was going to make another suicide attempt, he was sent to the medical unit, again. Two weeks later he convinced a social worker assigned to the jail that he was okay. That he had accepted his fate. He had settled into new life at Nashua Street, he told the social worker.

By all accounts, Philip Markoff has done just that. Reclassified in general population, he plays cards in a two-piece navy blue prison uniform. He counts among his buddies fellow accused killers, men like him who are suspected of flying into an uncontrollable rage and murdering defenseless women. "He gets along good with the scumbags," remarked one deputy sheriff. "He's fitting in now. Where he was nervous before, he is no longer nervous."

He has taken up chess. Everyone on his block plays a pretty mean game of poker now. In fact, Markoff was still good at gambling. So good that he ended up pissing off some of his fellow cellmates. And how do scumbags get back at other scumbags? They rat.

"Phil has a high IQ. Let's face it. Some of the other mutts in there with him do not. He was killing them in chess and checkers and cards. Someone got mad because Phil was taking cigarettes and canteen cash and ratted him out about the booze he was making in his cell," said a law enforcement official who saw the paperwork on Markoff's latest stint in the segregation unit.

That came in December of 2009. By then he had been in jail for eight months. He had settled into a routine of playing cards, checkers and chess. He got along with the other lowlifes. Deputy sheriffs charged with monitoring him were so grateful he had apparently stopped trying to kill himself that they didn't notice that he was starting to hoard fruit in his cell. Besides, there were no rules against having apples under the bed. Or piles of orange peels. Maybe he liked the smell. He was a big guy. Maybe he was going to get hungry. What did not occur to the deputy sheriffs, who were understaffed and charged with maintaining order among some of the most notorious accused killers in the entire state, was that Markoff was a guy who knew a little about the chemical makeup of things. After all, he was a standout medical student at one of the best schools in the nation. He had taken out loans to the tune of $130,000 to pay for it—cash that would certainly be eaten by the taxpayer, just like his legal bills were already being picked up by the Massachusetts taxpayer. And John Salsberg did not come cheap either. That investment almost paid off for Markoff when he devised a method to escape the hell of his new life with a bit of chemically induced relief.

The hoarded fruit was going to provide a way for Markoff to make a homemade moonshine, or "hooch" as he called it. He was letting the fruit rot in his room and then heating the rotten fruit in a plastic container against the vent in his cell. Sometimes he was brazen enough to walk to the canteen on his floor and microwave the bruised, rotten fruit hoping that the fermentation would create alcohol. It wouldn't taste very good. In fact, in some cases drinking that swill could even kill a person. But hell, who was worried about taste? He certainly was not. And dying would be a welcome reprieve from what Phil Markoff was facing in the coming months and years.

More is coming out, he told his brother. He knew it, too. And he also knew about the woman from New Bedford who had called prosecutors to tell them that she too could have encountered the man that had been dubbed "The Craigslist Killer." Investigators were not saying much about that call, but Markoff's attorney had certainly asked him about it. Markoff was not surprised. He was overheard in jail telling people as much. "All kinds of broads are going to say that they met me, that I tried to do them, too," he said. "Might be true. Might not be true."

Certainly it was not making Salsberg's job any easier. But then again, Salsberg was used to difficult clients. He would not be thwarted. Sure, it was frustrating when his client was sent back to the segregated unit, known as the suicide cellblock, where he was under twenty-three-hour-a-day lockdown for ten days. Salsberg barely noticed. He was busy defending a family, that's right, a family of drug dealers from Dorchester, a hardscrabble neighborhood in Boston. He got them off, as usual, despite the evidence that the feds had presented in the case.

The booze incident led Markoff to be written up for "violation of conduct code." *Big fucking deal*, he would tell his fellow scumbags over a Christmas dinner, which amounted to donated sliced ham and cold apple pie. *Big fucking deal. These fucking idiots don't know shit. And I will get the motherfucker who ratted me out.*

He wasn't just full of braggadocio. He really wasn't worried. He even mouthed off to the deputy sheriffs:

"With what they have on me, do you think I give a fuck about a little hooch?"

The shy, scared, acne-marked accused murderer who shuffled into the Nashua Street jail in April 2009 had turned into an arrogant con by the start of 2010. He was mouthy. He was brazen. And he had a little crew of card players that he ripped off on a daily basis. He didn't have to worry about his friends and family filling his canteen card. He would just take the candy and cookies that were paid for by the losers in his card games.

Markoff didn't even have court appearances to